AN OFFICER OF VERY EXTRAORDINARY MERIT

Charles Porterfield
and the
American War for Independence

1775-1780

Michael Cecere

HERITAGE BOOKS
2004

HERITAGE BOOKS

AN IMPRINT OF HERITAGE BOOKS, INC.

Books, CDs, and more—Worldwide

For our listing of thousands of titles see our website
at
www.HeritageBooks.com

Published 2004 by
HERITAGE BOOKS, INC.
Publishing Division
65 East Main Street
Westminster, Maryland 21157-5026

OTHER BOOKS BY THE AUTHOR:
THEY BEHAVED LIKE SOLDIERS:
Captain John Chilton and the Third Virginia Regiment, 1775-1778

International Standard Book Number: 0-7884-3223-0

Contents

Maps

Acknowledgments

My thanks go out to a number of people. First, to my wife, Susan, and our children, Jenny and Michael, thank you for your support and encouragement. The same goes to my parents, Paul and Teresa, who remain my biggest fans. I am also appreciative to my colleagues and students at Robert E. Lee High School. Their enthusiasm and interest in my work is a great motivator. Marguerite Knickmeyer, my teaching partner, and friend, deserves a big thank you as does Dave McKissack, who suggested Colonel Porterfield as a subject and helped in the editing. Lastly, I'd like to express my appreciation to the Simpson Library at Mary Washington College, the Handley Regional Library in Winchester, and the Central Rappahannock Regional Library in Fredericksburg, for their assistance and invaluable resources. The historical treasures kept in such libraries are windows to our past.

Introduction

Charles Porterfield was one of many patriots who helped secure America's independence. He was one of the first Virginians to join the American army at Boston in 1775. He endured a grueling march to Quebec, through the wilderness of Maine, and stormed the city's walls in a blinding snowstorm. After eight months of captivity, he rejoined the American effort, and commanded a company of men in Daniel Morgan's 11th Virginia Regiment.

In 1777, Captain Porterfield served in a select corps of light infantry. He saw heavy action at Cooches Bridge and Brandywine. He returned to his regiment, in October, and fought with them at Germantown. He also endured the hardships of Valley Forge.

In 1778, following the battle of Monmouth, Porterfield was appointed Major of a state regiment in Virginia. He left the continental army in 1779 to assume his new command. Aside from a promotion to Lieutenant Colonel of the state regiment, however, the next twelve months were relatively uneventful. This changed in 1780, when the British moved against Charleston, South Carolina. In April, 1780, Lieutenant Colonel Porterfield led a relief detachment to the besieged city.

This was his last service for the American cause. On August 16th, Colonel Porterfield was grievously wounded at the battle of Camden. He was captured by the British and paroled, but his wound was so severe that he was unable to leave the area. After months of suffering, Lieutenant Colonel Porterfield succumbed to his injuries.

Charles Porterfield lies somewhere in South Carolina, in a grave known only to God. Like many of his men, Colonel Porterfield devoted five years of his life, and made the ultimate sacrifice, for a cause that too many people take for granted. Men who gave as much as they, deserve to be remembered. This then, is their story. The story of one forgotten patriot, and the men who served with him.

Chapter One

To Arms! To Arms!

Virginia, like all of the American colonies, was abuzz with excitement in the spring of 1775. In late March, Patrick Henry, as only he could do, inflamed passions with his plea to, "Give Me Liberty or Give Me Death." Three weeks later, on April 19th, fighting erupted in Massachusetts when British troops marched on Concord. The Massachusetts militia responded with vigor and pursued the British back to Boston. Just two days later, Virginia's Royal Governor, Lord Dunmore, created his own crisis, by transferring a large supply of the colony's gunpowder, from the powder magazine in Williamsburg, to a British ship anchored in the James River. Few people believed Dunmore's explanation, that he was securing the gunpowder from a possible slave insurrection. Instead, most saw the act as an attempt to disarm the colony.

Within a week, a thousand armed and angry Virginians gathered in Fredericksburg to march on the capital and demand the gunpowder's return. Before they embarked, however, news arrived of Dunmore's offer to pay for the powder. Although this temporarily defused the crisis, Virginia remained on edge.

As summer approached, war drums continued to beat. In Massachusetts, a large army of New England troops kept the British confined to Boston. In Philadelphia, the Second Continental Congress voted to assume control of this army and appointed George Washington its commander. And in Virginia, men mustered and drilled with their local militia units in preparation for war.

The Reverend Philip Fithian, traveling through Winchester, Virginia on June 6th, witnessed these activities. He wrote in his journal that,

"*Mars, the great God of Battle, is now honoured in every Part of this spacious Colony but here* [Winchester] *every Presence is warlike, every Sound is martial! Drums beating, Fifes & Bag-Pipes playing, & only sonorous & heroic Tunes—Every Man has a hunting-shirt, which is the Uniform of each Company—Almost all have a Cockade, & bucktale in their Hatts, to represent that they are hardy, resolute, & invincible Natives of the Woods of America.*" [1]

Fithian also noted that the Frederick County Committee passed the following resolve.

"*...every Member of this County, between sixteen, & sixty years of Age, shall appear once every Month, at least, in the Field under Arms; & it is recommended to all to muster weekly for their Improvement.*"[2]

This martial spirit was still evident ten days later, when Fithian again visited Winchester. On June 17th he wrote,

"*This Town in Arms. All in a Hunting-Shirt uniform & Bucks Tale in their Hats. Indeed they make a grand Figure.*"[3]

Perhaps Fithian observed Winchester's reaction to news that the Continental Congress had voted to raise two companies of Virginia riflemen. Two other rifle companies

---

[1] Philip Fithian, *Philip Vickers Fithian: Journal, 1775-1776, Written on the Virginia-Pennsylvania Frontier and in the Army Around New York*, Edited by Robert Albion and Leonidas Dodson (Princeton: Princeton University Press, 1934), 24
[2] Ibid. 25
[3] Ibid. 31

were raised in Maryland and six more in Pennsylvania. They were all ordered to march to Boston as soon as possible and serve as light infantry.[4]

Frederick County acted quickly to recruit a rifle company. On June 22nd, the County Committee unanimously appointed Daniel Morgan as captain. Morgan's commission read in part,

> *"In obedience to a resolve of the Continental Congress...this committee, reposing a special trust in the courage, conduct, and reverence for liberty under the spirit of the British constitution, of Daniel Morgan, Esq., do hereby certify that we have unanimously appointed him to command a Virginia company of riflemen to march from this county. He is hereby directed to act, by exercising the officers and soldiers under his command, taking particular care to provide them with the necessaries, as the 1st Resolves of Congress directs..."[5]*

This appointment was soon confirmed by a commission from Congress.[6]

Captain Morgan started recruiting immediately, hoping to get a jump on Hugh Stephenson, captain of the other Virginian rifle company. Henry Bedinger, a member of Stephenson's company, noted that,

---

[4] *Journals of the Continental Congress*, 14 June, 1775, Library of Congress Online at www.loc.gov

[5] James Graham, *Life of General Daniel Morgan,* (Bloomingburg, NY: Zebrowski: Historical Services Publishing Co., 1993), 53 (Originally published in 1856)

[6] Ibid. The commission, also dated June 22, 1775, read, "We, reposing especial trust and confidence in your patriotism, valor, conduct, and fidelity, do, by these presents, constitute and appoint you to be Captain of a company of riflemen in the army of the United Colon'es, raised for the defence of American Liberty, and for repelling every hostile invasion thereof."

"Great exertions were made by each Captain to complete his company first, that merit might be claimed on that account. Volunteers presented themselves from every direction, in the vicinity of these Towns; [Winchester and Shepherdstown] *none were received but young men of Character, and of sufficient property to Clothe themselves completely, find their own arms, and accoutrements, that is, an approved Rifle, handsome shot pouch, and powder-horn, blanket, knapsack, with such decent clothing as should be prescribed, but which was at first ordered to be only a Hunting shirt and pantaloons, fringed on every edge, and in Various ways. Our Company was raised in less than a week. Morgan had equal success."*[7]

"I recruited 96 men in a few days," Morgan proudly recalled years later.[8] Men flocked to Winchester, willing to commit a year of their lives to defend their threatened liberties in far off Boston.

"So great was the enthusiasm of the moment," recalled Peter Bruin, one of Morgan's first recruits, *"that the difficulty did not depend on raising the number of men required but in selecting from those who crowded to the standard for admission, so that but a short time was employed in mustering and equiping the company."*[9]

---

[7] Henry Bedinger to --- Findley, in Danske Dandridge, *Historic Shepherdstown,* (Charlottesville, VA: Michie Co., 1910), 79
[8] "General Daniel Morgan, An Autobiography", *The Historical Magazine and Notes and Queries Concerning the Antiquities, History and Biography of America, 2nd Series Vol. 9* (1871), 379
[9] Peter Bruin Pension Application, in *Virginia Revolutionary Pension Applications, Vol. 12,* ed. John Dorman, (Washington, D.C.: 1965), 3

Twenty-five year old Charles Porterfield was typical of the men selected for the rifle company. Born in Frederick County in 1750, he was over six feet tall and possessed a quiet, serious demeanor.[10] He apparently came from a family of financial means, for later in the war he raised, and equipped, a company of men, largely at his own expense.[11] Porterfield served as a cadet in Morgan's rifle company. Cadets were often referred to as gentlemen volunteers. Although they held no official rank, their status as "officers in training" placed them just below lieutenants and ensigns in the unit hierarchy.

The men of Morgan's rifle company were all excellent shots, the "marksmen" of their day. In an age when most soldiers used smoothbore muskets, with an effective range of 50 to 100 yards, experienced riflemen could consistently hit their mark at more than 200 yards. The advantage that rifles had in accuracy, however, was somewhat negated by their lower rate of fire. Musket-men, using pre-rolled cartridges containing powder and ball, could fire up to four rounds a minute. Riflemen, on the other hand, typically measured each charge from a powder horn. Furthermore, achieving the greater accuracy of a spinning projectile, as created by the rifle's grooved barrel, meant that a tight fitting lead ball, wrapped in a greased cloth patch, had to be forced down the barrel. As a result, it typically took riflemen two to three times longer to load their weapon. Another disadvantage of rifles was that, in most cases, bayonets could not be attached to them. Thus, in close combat situations, riflemen found themselves at a distinct disadvantage to their bayonet wielding enemy.

---

[10] Dudley Guilford, "A Sketch of the Military Services Performed by Guilford Dudley, Then of the Town of Halifax, North Carolina, During the Revolutionary War", Charles Campbell, ed., *Southern Literary Messenger, Vol. 11*, Issues 3-6, (1845), 147, 231
Obtained via the following website: http://battleofcamden.org/dudley.htm
[11] T. K. Cartmell, *Shenandoah Valley Pioneers and Their Descendants: A History of Frederick County, Virginia*, (Winchester, VA, 1909), 103

At first, this disadvantage was not very obvious. In fact, many believed that riflemen would be decisive in a conflict. Richard Henry Lee, writing about his fellow Virginia riflemen, stated that,

> *"This one County of Fincastle can furnish 1000 Rifle Men that for their number make the most formidable light Infantry in the World. The six frontier Counties can produce 6000 of these Men who from their amazing hardihood, their method of living so long in the woods without carrying provisions with them, the exceeding quickness with which they can march to distant parts, and above all, the dexterity to which they have arrived in the use of the Rifle Gun. There is not one of these Men who wish a distance less than 200 yards or a larger object than an Orange. – Every shot is fatal."*[12]

John Adams was also encouraged by the reputation of the riflemen. On June 18th, 1775 he optimistically wrote to his wife.

> *These* [riflemen] *are said to be all exquisite marksmen, and by means of the excellence of their firelocks, as well as their skill in the use of them, to send sure destruction to great distances.*[13]

[12] James C. Ballagh, ed., *Letters of Richard Henry Lee, Vol. 1* (New York: Macmillan Co., 1911), 130-131 (Richard Henry Lee to Arthur Lee, 24 February, 1775)
[13] John Adams to Elbridge Gerry, 18 June, 1775, *in Letters of Delegates to Congress, Vol. 1* (Aug. 1774 – Aug. 1775, Library of Congress: Online)

"Come Boys, Who's For Cambridge"

It took three weeks for Porterfield and the rest of Morgan's men to prepare for the long march north.[14]   They departed Winchester on July 14th, reaching Shepherdstown, Maryland by nightfall.[15]   Three days later, local militia companies escorted them through Frederick, Maryland, *"amidst the acclamation of all the inhabitants that attended them."*[16]   One observer noted in a letter that,

> *"On Monday last, July 17th, Capt. Morgan, from Virginia, with his company of riflemen (all chosen), marched through this place on their way to Boston. Their appearance was truly martial; their spirits amazingly elated; breathing nothing but a desire to join the American army and to engage the enemies of American liberties..."*[17]

Their reception in Frederick was typical of nearly every community they marched through. All along the route the men were greeted as heroes. Occasionally they halted to demonstrate their military skills. These stops were brief, however, because they had over 600 miles to cover. Captain Morgan set a rapid pace, averaging thirty miles a day. On July 24th they passed through Bethlehem, Pennsylvania.[18]   Three days later, at Sussex Court House, New Jersey, they fell in with a company of Pennsylvania riflemen. The Virginians

---

[14] Don Higginbotham, *Daniel Morgan: Revolutionary* Rifleman, (Chapel Hill: Univ. of North Carolina Press, 1961), 23
[15] Cartmell, 102
[16] Ibid.
[17] Dandridge, 95
[18] John W. Jordan, ed., "Bethleham During the Revolution," *Pennsylvania Magazine of History and Biography, Vol. 12* (1888), 387

soon outpaced the Pennsylvanians however, arriving at Cambridge on August 6th.[19]

The arrival of the rifle companies caused a big stir in the American camp. Riflemen were largely unknown in New England and their appearance, and reputation, made quite an impression. An unidentified American officer described the riflemen in a letter home.

> *"You will think me vain should I tell you how much the Riflemen are esteemed. Their dress, their arms, their size, strength and activity, but above all their eagerness to attack the enemy, entitle them to the first rank. The hunting shirt is like a full suit at St. James's. A Rifleman in his dress may pass sentinels and go almost where he pleases, while officers of other Regiments are stopped."[20]*

Surgeon's Mate James Thacher, of Massachusetts, was equally impressed, describing the riflemen as,

> *"remarkably stout and hardy men; many of them exceeding six feet in height. They are dressed in white frocks, or rifle-shirts, and round hats. These men are remarkable for the accuracy of their aim; striking a mark with great certainty at two hundred yards distance. At a review, a company of them, while on a quick advance, fired their balls into objects of seven inches diameter, at a distance of two hundred and fifty yards. They are now stationed on our lines, and their shot have frequently proved fatal to British officers and soldiers who expose*

---

[19] B. Floyd Flickinger, "Captain Morgan and His Riflemen," *Winchester-Frederick County Historical Society Journal, Vol. 14*, (2002), 56-57
[20] Ibid. 58-59

themselves to view, even at more than double the distance of common musket-shot." [21]

The deadly aim of the riflemen was also noticed by the enemy. The London Chronicle reported that American riflemen have, *"rifles particularly adapted to take off the officers of a whole line..."* [22] Another London newspaper wrote that, *"...with their cursed twisted gun, [riflemen are] the most fatal widow and orphan makers in the world."* [23]

An observer in the American camp noted that, *"since the riflemen arrived, they have killed six or eight officers of distinction."* [24] Even General Washington, in a letter to Congress, noted the impact of the riflemen.

> *" I last Saturday Evening ordered some of the Riflemen down to make a Discovery, or bring off a Prisoner...Since that Time we have on each side drawn in our sentries and there have been scattering Fires along the Lines. This Evening we have heard of three Captains who have been taken off by the Rifle Men..."* [25]

The British responded to the deadly fire of the riflemen with a lot more caution in their lines. Soon, Porterfield and his fellow Virginians had few targets to shoot at. The monotony of camp life and guard duty set in, and the riflemen

---

[21] James Thacher, M.D., *Military Journal of the American Revolution,* (Gansevoort, New York: Corner House Historical Publications, 1998), 31

[22] Richard B. LaCrosse Jr., *The Frontier Rifleman,* (Union City, TN: Pioneer Press, 1989), 83

[23] Ibid. 81

[24] Margaret Willard, ed., *Letters on the American Revolution: 1774-1776,* (Boston & New York: Houghton Mifflin Co., 1925), 185

[25] General Washington to John Hancock, 4 August, 1775, in *The Papers of George Washington: Revolutionary War Series, Vol. 1, June – September 1775,* ed. Philander D. Chase, (Charlottesville: University Press of Virginia, 1985), 226

grew restless. Discipline deteriorated, fights erupted, and the men grumbled at their inactivity. Not surprisingly, when rumors of an expedition to Canada circulated in camp, many riflemen volunteered to go.

Chapter Two

Quebec

The Plan

The plan was risky, bold, and secret. Since mid August, General Washington had pondered the idea of attacking Canada. British rule was tenuous, their small garrison stretched thin. Furthermore, the predominantly French Catholic population resented their presence. Washington hoped that this resentment might induce Canadians to join an attack on the British.[1]

On August 20th, General Washington shared his plan with General Philip Schuyler, the commander of American troops at Fort Ticonderoga.

"[I wish to] *communicate to you a Plan of an Expedition, which has engaged my Thoughts for several Days. It is to penetrate into Canada by way of the Kennebeck River, and so to Quebeck...I can very well spare a Detachment for this Purpose of one Thousand or twelve Hundred Men...If you are resolved to proceed...*[with] an attack from the direction of Lake Champlain] *it would make a Diversion that would distract Carlton* [the British Governor in Canada]...*He must either break up and follow this Party to Quebeck, by which he will leave you a free Passage, or he must suffer that important place to fall into our Hands, an Event, which would*

---

[1] Stephen Clark, *Following Their Footsteps: A Travel Guide & History of the 1775 Secret Expedition to Capture Quebec*, (Clark Books, 2003), 5

11

have a decisive Effect and influence on the publick Interest.[2]

The decision to proceed with the two pronged attack was left to General Schuyler. *"You will therefore by Return of this Messenger inform me of your ultimate Resolution"*, wrote Washington.[3]

It took six days for General Washington's message to reach General Schuyler and another six for Schuyler's affirmative reply to return to Boston.

> *"The Inclosed Information"*, wrote Schulyer, *"leaves no trace of doubt on my mind as to the propriety of going into Canada...And I have Accordingly... requested Gen: Montgomery to get every thing in the best readiness he could...The force I shall carry is far short of what I would wish. I believe It will not Exceed Seventeen Hundred men, and this will be a body Insufficient to Attempt Quebec [alone]...Should the detachment of Your body penetrate Into Canada and we meet with Success, Quebec must Inevitably fall into our hands...*[4]

Schuyler's reply prompted General Washington to set his plan in motion. First, he arranged the necessary transports for the expedition. On September 2nd, he wrote to Nathaniel Tracy, a merchant in the coastal town of Newburyport, Massachusetts, authorizing him to, *"take up for the Service of*

---

[2] General Washington to Major General Philip Schuyler, 20 August, 1775 in *The Papers of George Washington, Vol. 1,* 332

[3] Ibid.

[4] General Schuyler to General Washington, 27 August, 1775 in *The Papers of George Washington, Vol. 1,* 368

the said Colonies so many Vessels as shall be necessary for transporting from this Army on a secret Expedition."[5]

The next day, Washington ordered Reuben Colburn, the owner of a small shipyard and sawmill in Gardinerstown, Maine, to proceed, *"with all Expedition and without delay... [with] the Construction of Two Hundred Batteaus."*[6] These craft, designed to haul cargo on lakes and rivers, were needed to transport supplies up the Kennebec River. Colburn was ordered to take twenty men with him to assist in the construction of the boats. He was also told to procure as much pork and flour as possible from the local inhabitants.[7]

Two days later, General Washington issued orders to form the detachment. He placed Colonel Benedict Arnold, of Connecticut, in command.

"A Detachment consisting of two Lieut. Colonels, two Majors, ten Captains, thirty Subalterns, thirty Serjeants, thirty Corporals, four Drummers, two Fifers, and six hundred and seventy six privates; to parade to morrow morning at eleven O' Clock, upon the Common, in Cambridge, to go upon Command with Col. Arnold of Connecticut; one Company of Virginia Rifle-men and two Companies from Col. Thompson's Pennsylvania Regiment of Rifle-men, to parade at the same time and place, to join the above Detachment. Tents and Necessaries proper and convenient for the whole, will be supplied by the Quarter Master Genl. immediately upon the Detachment being collected"[8]

---

[5] General Washington to Nathaniel Tracy, 2 September, 1775 in *The Papers of George Washington, Vol. 1*, 404-405

[6] General Washington to Reuben Colburn, 3 September, 1775, in *The Papers of George Washington, Vol. 1*, 471

[7] Ibid.

[8] General Orders, 5 September, 1775 , *in The Papers of George Washington, Vol. 1*, 473

Washington's orders further specified that only men who, *"are active Woodsmen, and well acquainted with bateaus,"* should volunteer for this service.[9]

It took a few days for the detachment to assemble at Cambridge. Totaling nearly 1,100 men, it was divided into ten musket and three rifle companies.[10] Charles Porterfield, and the rest of Morgan's Virginians – easily meeting Washington's standards for service – made up one of the rifle companies. In fact, Captain Morgan assumed overall command of the rifle detachment.

On September 11th, the rifle companies began a forty-five mile march to Newburyport, arriving two days later. They spent the next five days waiting for the transports to be loaded and the remainder of the detachment to arrive. The entire expedition finally boarded ships on September 18th and set sail for the Kennebec River the next morning. According to Abner Stocking, a private in one of the musket companies, the expedition departed with some fanfare. *"Many pretty Girls stood upon the shore, I suppose weeping for the departure of their sweethearts."*[11]

The March

The expedition arrived, somewhat scattered, at Colburn's shipyard, on September 22nd. Supplies were transferred from the ships to the waiting bateaux, and the expedition continued upriver to Fort Western. The fort, which still stands in present day Augusta, was built in 1754 during the French and Indian

---

[9] Ibid.
[10] Clark, 9
[11] Kenneth Roberts, *March to Quebec: Journals of the Members of Arnold's Expedition*, (New York: Country Life Press, 1938), 546 (Abner Stocking's Journal)

War. It was the base camp for the expedition, the place where final preparations for the long trip upriver were made.

Colonel Arnold, hoping to avoid bottlenecks along some of the narrow portage passages of the river, split the expedition into four divisions, with four different departure times. The first division, consisting of the three rifle companies, was commanded by Captain Morgan.[12] They began the trek northward on September 25th.

They were not the first to head upriver however. Two small scouting parties, using birch bark canoes, departed on September 23rd. These lightweight craft were well suited for the shallow waters of the Kennebec. As a result, they averaged almost twenty miles a day.[13]

It was much harder, however, for the main detachments of the expedition. As each division left Fort Western, they struggled to propel the heavy bateaux through the rocky shoals of the river. Two days into the trip, Private Caleb Haskell noted in his journal,

"We begin to see that we have a scene of trouble to go through in this river, the water is swift and the shoal full of rocks, ripples, and falls, which oblige us to wade a great part of the way."[14]

Pennsylvania rifleman George Morison, serving in Morgan's division, gave a similar description, writing that,

"The water in many places being so shallow, that we were often obliged to haul the boats after us through rock and shoals, frequently up to our middle and over our

---

[12] Clark, 31

[13] Roberts, 303 (Joseph Henry Journal)

[14] Roberts, 474 (Caleb Haskell Journal)

heads in the water; and some of us with difficulty escaped being drowned."[15]

While the men in the bateaux struggled with the swift current and rocky shoals, the rest of the expedition struggled through the woods alongside the river. They were frequently called upon to assist with the boats, especially when difficult rapids or waterfalls were encountered. Just four days into the trip, Abner Stocking noted that,

> "*This day (September 29th) we arrived to the second carrying place...*[present day Skowhegan, Maine] *it occasioned much delay and great fatigue. We had to ascend a ragged rock, near on 100 feet in height and almost perpendicular. Though it seemed as though we could hardly ascend it without any burden, we succeeded in dragging our bateaus and baggage up it.*"[16]

The weather also proved a challenge, turning cold and raw. Captain Simeon Thayer noted on September 30th that, "*Last night, our clothes being wet, were frozen a pane of glass thick, which proved very disagreeable, being obliged to lie in them.*"[17]

The expedition struggled onward, its divisions strung out for miles along the river. On October 7th, Porterfield, and the rest of the rifle division, reached the Great Carrying Place. This was the location of a twelve mile portage route used by Indians to connect the Kennebec and Dead Rivers. Three ponds linked the route, making the overland trek a bit easier. Nevertheless, hauling the heavy boats and supplies over the rough terrain was still a daunting task. The riflemen were

---

[15] Roberts, 511 (George Morison Journal)
[16] Roberts, 548 (Abner Stocking Journal)
[17] Roberts, 250 (Simon Thayer Journal)

given the added responsibility of clearing and improving the path for the detachments to come. Rifleman George Morison described the difficulties they endured.

"This morning we hauled out our Batteaux from the river and carried thro' brush and mire, over hills and swamps...to a pond which we crossed, and encamped for the night. This transportation occupied us three whole days, during which time we advanced but five miles. This was by far the most fatiguing movement that had yet befell us. The rains had rendered the earth a complete bog; insomuch that we were often half leg deep in the mud, stumbling over all fallen logs...Our encampments these two last nights were almost insupportable; for the ground was so soaked with rain that the driest situation we could find was too wet to lay upon any length of time; so that we got but little rest. Leaves to bed us could not be obtained and we amused ourselves around our fires most all the night...The incessant toil we experienced in ascending the river, as well as the still more fatiguing method of carrying our boats, laden with the provisions, camp equipage etc., from place to place, might have subdued the resolution of men less patient and less persevering than we were."[18]

After days of backbreaking work, the riflemen reached the Dead River. They hoped that the deeper waters of this river meant easier travel ahead. And in fact, for a few days, the expedition made good progress. The weather deteriorated again, however, and the expedition was forced to halt for four days and endure the remnants of a hurricane. Rifleman Joseph Henry described the storm's impact.

---

[18] Roberts, 513-514 (George Morison Journal)

"...a most heavy torrent of rain fell upon us, which continued all night...towards morning we were awakened by the water that flowed in upon us from the river. We fled to high ground. When morning came, the river presented a most frightful aspect: it had risen at least eight feet, and flowed with terrifying rapidity. None but the most strong and active boatmen entered the boats. The army marched on the south side of the river, making large circuits to avoid the overflowing (river)...This was one of the most fatiguing marches we had as yet performed, though the distance was not great in a direct line. But having no path, and being necessitated to climb the steepest hills and without food, for we took none with us, thinking the boats would be near us all day.[19]

To make matters worse, it was also discovered that much of the food stores had spoiled. Surgeon Isaac Senter noted,

"The bread casks not being water-proof, admitted the water in plenty, swelled the bread, burst the casks, as well as soured the whole bread. The same fate attended a number of fine casks of peas. These with the others were condemned. We were now curtailed of a very valuable and large part of our provisions...Our fare was now reduced to salt pork and flour. Beef we had now and then, when we could purchase a fat creature, but that was seldom. A few barrels of salt beef remained on hand, but of so indifferent quality, as scarce to be eaten, being killed in the heat of summer, took much damage after salting, that rendered it not only very unwholesome, but very unpalatable."[20]

---

[19] Roberts, 330 (Joseph Henry Journal)
[20] Roberts, 203 (Isaac Senter Journal)

Despite the difficult conditions, the expedition continued onward. On October 25th, a heavy snowfall hit the men, adding to their misery. Dr. Isaac Senter reported that,

> *"Every prospect of distress now came thundering on with a two fold rapidity. A storm of snow had covered the ground nigh six inches deep, attended with very severe weather."*[21]

Private Morison reported a similar situation, noting in his journal that, *"Last night there fell a heavy snow, and this morning it blew up cold; we suffered considerably this day."*[22]

When the riflemen reached the area known as the Height of Land (the highest point of the march) the two Pennsylvania companies abandoned all but one of their bateaux. The Virginians, however, at Morgan's command, carried their remaining seven boats over this difficult portage. Joseph Henry described how the Virginians struggled to haul the boats overland.

> *"It would have made your heart ache to view the intolerable labors of these fine fellows. Some of them, it was said, had the flesh worn from their shoulders, even to the bone."*[23]

Porterfield and his fellow Virginians were not alone in their suffering, however. The great physical exertions and lack of provisions took its toll on all the men. George Morison reported that,

> *"The time had now arrived when our suffering began to assume a different shape. Famine stared us in the*

---

[21] Roberts, 210 (Isaac Senter Journal)
[22] Roberts, 517-518 (George Morison Journal)
[23] Roberts, 335-336 (Joseph Henry Journal)

face. Our provisions began to grow scarce, many of our men too sick, and the whole of us much reduced by our fatigues. "[24]

A week later, Morison recorded in his journal that,

> *"Never perhaps was there a more forlorn set of human beings...Every one of us shivering from head to foot, as hungry as wolves, and nothing to eat save a little flour we had left, which we made dough of and baked in the fires...*"[25]

Private Henry noted that the situation was so desperate that,

> *"the men were told by the officers that order would not be required in the march – each one must put their best foot foremost."*[26]

In other words, it was now every man for himself. Dr. Senter confirmed the desperate situation, writing on November 1st that,

> *"We had now arrived...to almost the zenith of distress. Several had been entirely destitute of either meat or bread for many days...The voracious disposition many of us had now arrived at, rendered almost anything admissible...In company was a poor dog, [who had] hitherto lived through all the tribulations...This poor animal was instantly devoured, without leaving any vestige of the sacrifice. Nor did the shaving soap, pomatum, and even the lip*

---

[24] Roberts, 515-516 (George Morison Journal)
[25] Roberts, 524 (George Morison Journal)
[26] Roberts, 336 (Joseph Henry Journal)

salve, leather of their shoes, cartridge boxes, &c.,
share any better fate... "[27]

The expedition had degenerated into a disorganized band of emaciated men, scattered along a twenty mile stretch of land. Many men fell out of the march, resigned to die in the wilderness. The last three musket companies of the column actually turned back, without orders. Yet, Porterfield, and the rest of the expedition, carried on.

Then, on November 3rd, the front of the column sighted a small herd of cattle being driven towards them. It was an American advance party with desperately needed provisions from the local inhabitants. The expedition had made it out of the wilderness! They had survived six weeks of hardship and misery, completing one of the most difficult marches in American military history. The desperately needed cattle were immediately butchered and the famished men gorged themselves on fresh beef and other provisions. Rejuvenated by this new found nourishment, many returned to the wilderness to assist their exhausted comrades. Arnold's march through the wilderness was over, but more challenges lay ahead.

Siege of Quebec

A few days after emerging from the wilderness, Arnold's force came within sight of their objective, Quebec. The city was ill prepared for an attack, mustering just over a thousand men to defend the large fortress.[28]

On the evening of November 14th, the bulk of Arnold's force, approximately five hundred men, crossed the St. Lawrence River. According to Captain Daniel Morgan,

---

[27] Roberts, 218-219 (Isaac Senter Journal)
[28] Robert Hatch, *Thrust for Canada: The American Attempt on Quebec in 1775-76*, (Boston: Houghton Mifflin, 1979), 113

> *"...we crossed the river in some small craft which we found drawn up in the guts, and some bark canoes, (which we purchased from the Indians,) we passed between two men of war, in point blank shot; but we slipped through, undiscovered."*[29]

Outnumbered two to one though, Colonel Arnold accepted a war council's recommendation to delay an attack. Instead, they commenced a siege of the city and waited for General Montgomery to arrive with re-enforcements and supplies. Colonel Arnold explained his actions in a letter to General Washington.

> *"...I passed the St. Lawrence without obstruction, except from a barge, into which we fired, and killed three men; but as the enemy were apprised of our coming and the garrison augmented to near seven hundred men, besides the inhabitants, it was not thought proper to storm the place, but cut off their communication with the country, until the arrival of Gen. Montgomery. We accordingly invested the town with about 550 men...We marched up several times near the walls, in hopes of drawing them out but to no effect, though they kept a constant cannonading and killed us one man."*[30]

A few days into the siege, news arrived that the enemy was preparing an attack of their own. An inventory of supplies revealed that the Americans were ill prepared.

[29] Henry B. Dawson, "General Daniel Morgan: An Autobiography" in *The Historical Magazine and Notes and Queries Concerning the Antiquities, History and Biography of America,* 2nd Series, *Vol. 9* (Morrisania, NY, 1871), 379

[30] Colonel Benedict Arnold to General George Washington, 20 November, 1775, in *The Papers of George Washington, Vol. 2,* 403

"I ordered a strict examination to be made into the state of our arms and ammunition," Colonel Arnold wrote to General Washington, *"when to my great surprise, I found many of our cartridges unfit for use (which in appearance were very good) and that we had no more than 5 rounds to each man. It was judged prudent in our situation not to hazard a battle."*[31]

As a result, the Americans withdrew to Point aux Tremble, twenty miles southwest of Quebec. This post proved very comfortable, and the men indulged themselves with plenty of food and cozy quarters. They also obtained much needed winter clothing.[32]

General Montgomery arrived on December 2nd with 300 men and additional supplies. Montgomery assumed command of the combined American force, which was still outnumbered, and returned to Quebec to resume the siege.[33] In a series of messages to Governor Carleton, General Montgomery boldly demanded the surrender of the fortress city. Carleton refused to entertain the notion. In frustration, General Montgomery commenced a bombardment of the city, but to little effect. It soon became apparent that an assault on the walled city was necessary to dislodge the enemy.

The Attack

General Montgomery's plan was to strike Quebec from two directions, while feigning an attack from a third. Montgomery would lead 300 New York troops toward the lower town from

---

[31] Ibid.

[32] Hatch, 117-118

[33] Colonel Benedict Arnold to General George Washington, 5 December, 1775, in *The Papers of George Washington, Vol. 2,* 495

the south. At the same time, small detachments would demonstrate in front of the western approaches to the town. Lastly, Colonel Arnold, with 600 men, would strike the lower town of Quebec from the north.[34] Once this section of the town was captured, the united American force would storm the upper town.

Since they were still outnumbered, the American plan depended on both surprise and decisive execution. The Americans waited for stormy weather, in the hope that it would provide more cover. They got their wish on December 30th, in the form of a blizzard.

Early in the morning of December 31st, with the storm still raging, the American army formed for battle. The attack began at 4:00 a.m. General Montgomery led his detachment to Wolf's Cove, and then marched along the St Lawrence riverbank towards the lower town. They were discovered by enemy sentries as they approached a barricade. The British fired a volley, killing General Montgomery instantly. The loss of their leader unnerved the Americans, and the detachment withdrew from the attack, leaving Arnold's detachment on its own.

Colonel Arnold's column, unaware of this setback, approached the gates of Quebec through the northern suburbs. Charles Porterfield recounted the attack in his diary.

> *"We paraded at 4 o' clock, A.M....The signal given, with shouts we set out. In passing by the Palace gate, they fired, and the bells rung an alarm. We marched with as much precipitancy as possible, sustaining a heavy fire for some distance, without the opportunity to return it, being close under the wall."[35]*

---

[34] Brendan Morrissey, *Quebec 1775: The American invasion of Canada,* (Osprey, 2003), 54-54

[35] Diary of Colonel Charles Porterfield, in *Magazine of American History, Vol. 21,* (April 1889), 318-319

Rifleman Joseph Henry gave a similar account of the approach.

> *"Covering the locks of our guns with the lappets of our coats, and holding down our heads, (for it was impossible to bear up our faces against the imperious storm of wind and snow,) we ran along the foot of the hill in single file...we received a tremendous fire of musketry from the ramparts above us. Here we lost some brave men, when powerless to return the salutes we received, as the enemy was covered by his impregnable defences. They were even sightless to us – we could see nothing but the blaze from the muzzles of their muskets."[36]*

Arnold's detachment continued on until it reached an enemy battery. The original plan called for an American field piece to be brought forth to engage the battery. Dragging the heavy cannon through the deep snow, however, proved too difficult and it was abandoned along the route. Complicating matters further, the main body of Arnold's force went astray in the narrow streets of the lower town. So when the American advance party approached the battery, their only immediate support was Captain Morgan's company of riflemen.

Charles Porterfield described what happened.

> *" Coming to the barrier of the entrance of the lower town, guarded by a captain and 50 men, with two pieces of cannon, one of which they discharged and killed two men, we forced them from the cannon, firing in at the port-holes, all the time exposed to the fire of the musketry from the bank above us in the upper town. Here, Colonel Arnold was wounded in*

---

[36] Roberts, 375-376 (Joseph Henry Journal)

the leg and had to retire. The scaling ladders being brought up, if there was any honor in being first over the barrier, I had it. I was immediately followed by Captain Morgan. Upon our approach the guards fled, and we followed close to the guard-house, when, making a halt till some more men should come up, we sallied through into the street. We took thirty men and a captain..."[37]

Daniel Morgan gave a similar account of the attack, with one notable exception. He placed Porterfield behind him as they scaled the barricade. With Colonel Arnold wounded and command falling upon him, Morgan recounted that,

"I had to attack a two-gun battery, supported by Captain M'Leod and 50 regular troops. The first gun that was fired missed us, the second flashed, when I ordered the ladder, which was on two men's shoulders, to be placed...I mounted myself, and was the first man who leaped into the town, among M'Leod's guard, who were panic struck, and, after a faint resistance, ran into a house that joined the battery and platform...Charles Porterfield, who was then a Cadet in my company, was the first man who followed me; the rest lost not a moment, but spring in as fast as they could find room; all this was performed in a few seconds. I ordered the men to fire into the house, and follow up their fire with their pikes (for besides our rifles we were furnished with long espontoons) this was done, and the guard was driven into the street. I went through a sally-port at the end of the platform; met them in the street; and ordered them to lay down their arms, if they expected

---

[37] Porterfield Diary, 319

quarter; they took me at my word and every man threw down his gun. "[38]

The Americans had broken through the first barricade, but in doing so, they were scattered about the lower town. A long delay ensued, as Morgan waited for the rest of the American force to arrive. *"We paraded for some time in the street,"* recalled Charles Porterfield. *"Here we continued for near an hour, before two hundred men got into the barrier, some without officers, and some officers without men, all in confusion..."* [39]

At the beginning of this delay, Captain Morgan advanced forward to reconnoiter the second barricade. He observed that, *"The sally-port through the barrier was standing open; the guard left it...I found no person in arms at all."* [40] Morgan returned to the first barricade and called a Council of War. He proposed that the small force immediately advance on the second barrier. According to Morgan,

> *"I was overruled by hard reasoning; it was stated that, if I went on, I would break an order, in the first place; in the next place, I had more prisoners than I had men; that if I left them, they might break out, retake the battery, and cut off our retreat; that General Montgomery was certainly coming down the River St. Lawrence, and would join us in a few minutes, so that we were sure of conquest if we acted with caution. To these arguments I sacrificed my own opinion and lost the town.* "[41]

---

[38] Dawson, 379-380 (Morgan Autobiography)
[39] Porterfield Diary, 319
[40] Dawson, 380 (Morgan Autobiography)
[41] Ibid.

Nearly an hour passed before the attack was resumed. During this delay, the enemy rushed men to the second barrier. As daylight approached, Morgan finally ordered his men forward. Charles Porterfield noted that,

> "*On approaching the second barrier,* [the enemy] *hailed us. We immediately fired; they returned it with a shower of shot. Being planted in houses on the opposite side of the barrier, a continual fire ensued for some time, while we rushed up to the barrier, set up our ladder, and, at the same instant, Captain Morgan mounted one, I the other, to force our way, spear in hand, but we were obliged to draw back. Here we were at a disadvantage. Our guns being wet, could not return the fire we were subject to;* [we] *were obliged to retreat into the street.*"[42]

Rifleman George Morison also described the assault on the second barricade.

> "*...the ladders are laid to the wall – our gallant officers are mounting followed by several men when a furious discharge of musketry is let loose upon us from behind houses; in an instant we are assailed from different quarters with a deadly fire. We now find it impossible to force the battery or guard the port-holes any longer. –We rush on to every part, rouse the enemy from their coverts, and force a body of them to an open fight, some of our riflemen take to houses and do considerable execution. We are now attacked by thrice our number; the battle becomes hot, and is much scattered; but we distinguish each other by hemlock springs previously placed in our hats. All our officers act most gallantly. Betwixt*

---

[42] Porterfield Diary, 319

every peal the awful voice of Morgan is heard, whose gigantic stature and terrible appearance carries dismay among the foe wherever he comes. "[43]

Despite Morgan's bold leadership, however, the American situation was critical. *"We are now attacked in our rear,"* wrote Morison, *"the enemy increase momentarily –they call out to us to surrender but we surrender them our bullets..."* [44] Charles Porterfield found cover inside a house where he, fellow Virginian Peter Bruin, and seven or eight other men continued the fight.

> *"We fired...from the windows,"* wrote Porterfield, *"determined to stand it out or die...Upon seeing Colonel Green and others give up their arms, we held a council what to do, Bruin declaring to the men that, if they thought proper to risk it, he was willing to fight our way out – that he should stand or fall with them."* [45]

While the fight raged at the second barrier, an enemy force of 500 men moved to retake the first one. They encountered Captain Henry Dearborn's company of musket-men, who, due to their wet weapons, were unable to offer much resistance. Dearborn surrendered his company, and control of the barricade. Morgan's retreat was now cut off.

Nevertheless, the Americans fought on, hoping that General Montgomery's force would arrive to relieve them. By 10:00 a.m., however, it was evident that the attack had failed, and that Morgan's men were trapped. Promised good treatment from their captors, they surrendered in small groups. Daniel Morgan was one of the last to do so, reportedly

---

[43] Roberts, 537 (Morison Journal)
[44] Ibid. 538
[45] Porterfield Diary, 319

weeping with anger as he handed his sword, not to the enemy, but to a local clergyman.[46] The battle of Quebec was over. Ahead lay eight months of captivity for the Virginians and their comrades.

Over four hundred Americans were captured at Quebec. Another hundred were killed or wounded.[47] The British lost only a handful of men. Yet, Governor Carleton refused to press his advantage and remained behind the city's walls. Colonel Arnold, once again in overall command due to General Montgomery's death, slowly recovered from his leg wound and brazenly kept his small force outside the walls of Quebec, daring the British to attack.

Inside Quebec, Morgan, Porterfield, and the other American captives faired reasonably well. Great kindness and consideration were shown the officers and men. Lieutenant William Heth, of Morgan's company, noted in his diary that,

> *"Many of the Gent. Officers waited upon us -- & promis'd to give what assistance they could...His Excellency* [Governor Carleton] *made us a Compliment of a Hogshead of exceeding good Porter...Rev. John Oliver Brian...presented us with 2 Hhds* [hogsheads or barrels] *Spanish wine, 6 Loav's sugar & 12 lb. Tea."*[48]

The Americans thanked the Reverend for his generosity, but kindly refused the tea.

Charles Porterfield, who grew seriously ill in May, experienced similar consideration. William Heth noted in his diary that,

---

[46] Graham, *Life of General Daniel Morgan,* 103

[47] Hatch, 140

[48] "Diary of Lieutenant William Heth while a Prisoner in Quebec, 1776", annotated by B. Floyd Flickinger in *Annual Papers of Winchester Virginia Historical Society, Vol. 1,* (1931), 39-40

"Doctor Maleen (Surgeon General) called this forenoon & acquainted Charly Porterfield (who is in a very low state of health) that he had applyd to the General for liberty to go into the county – but some inconvenience attending that, he would let him go home in the first Vessel that sailed for Halifax."[49]

It appeared, in fact, that Governor Carleton was disposed to let all the Americans return home.[50]

It was two more months, however, before this came to be. On August 7th, the American captives were finally granted their parole. They were allowed to return home with a promise not to take up arms until they were officially exchanged. Three days later, they boarded transports for New York, arriving on September 11th, 1776.[51] Their long ordeal was over, but the fight had just begun.

---

[49] Ibid. 61

[50] 'Diary of a Prisoner of War at Quebec, 1776" communicated by J.A. Waddell, *The Virginia Magazine of History and Biography, Vol. 9* (Richmond, VA: The Virginia Historical Society, July 1901 no. 1), 149

[51] Graham, 115

Arnold's March to Quebec

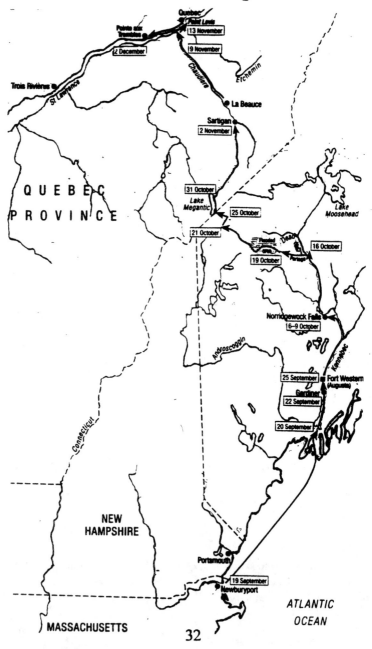

Quebec
Point Levis
13 November
9 November
Pointe aux
Trembles
2 December
Etchemin
Trois Rivières
St Lawrence
Chaudière
La Beauce
Sartigan
2 November
31 October
Lake
Megantic
25 October
Lake
Moosehead
21 October
Dead
Flooded
area
16 October
Portage
19 October
Norridgewock Falls
6–9 October
Androscoggin
Kennebec
25 September
Fort Western
(Augusta)
Gardiner
22 September
20 September

QUEBEC
PROVINCE

Connecticut

NEW
HAMPSHIRE

Portsmouth

19 September
Newburyport

ATLANTIC
OCEAN

MASSACHUSETTS

32

Quebec

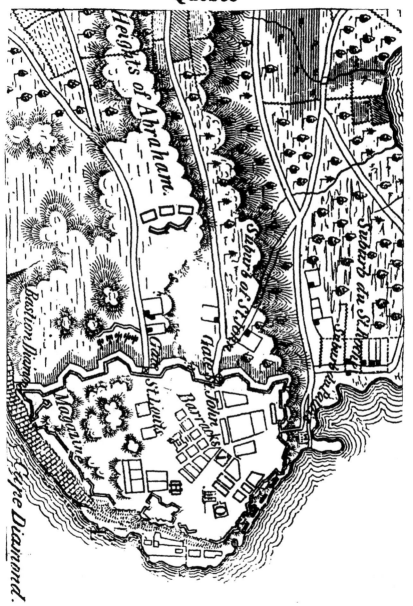

Chapter Three

The 11th Virginia

Charles Porterfield and his fellow Virginians reached home in October. Their fifteen month absence had been difficult on their families, as well as themselves. Many of the men were tired of war. And yet, the news from the north was bleak.

Chased from Brooklyn and Manhattan Island, the American army was rapidly disintegrating. The Continental Congress appealed for more troops, and Virginia responded by authorizing six additional regiments.[1] This brought the state's total number of continental regiments to fifteen.

Daniel Morgan's conduct at Quebec made him an obvious choice to command one of the new regiments. General Washington revealed his high regard for Morgan when, upon his return from Quebec, he recommended him for command of a special rifle battalion. This battalion, composed of independent rifle companies from Virginia, Pennsylvania, and Maryland, was originally commanded by Morgan's old rival, Colonel Hugh Stephenson. When Stephenson died of an illness, in September, 1776, command went to Lieutenant Colonel Moses Rawlings of Maryland. With Daniel Morgan's return to the army, however, a strong case was made that he should assume command of the rifle battalion. General Washington said as much in a letter to Congress on September 28th, 1776.

> *"As Col: Hugh Stephenson of the Rifle Regiment ordered lately to be raised, is dead...I would beg*

---

[1] William Hening, *The Statutes at Large Being a Collection of all the Laws of Virginia, Vol. 9* (Richmond: J & G Cochran, 1821), 179

leave to recommend to the particular notice of Congress, Captain Daniel Morgan, just returned among the prisoners from Canada, as a fit and proper person to succeed to the vacancy occasioned by his Death. The present Field Officers of the Regiment cannot claim any right in preference to him, because he ranked above them as Captain when he first entered the service; His Conduct as an Officer on the expedition with General Arnold last fall, his intrepid behavior in the Assault on Quebec when the brave Montgomery fell; the inflexible attachment he professed to our Cause during his imprisonment and which he perseveres in; added to these his residence in the place Col: Stevenson came from and his Interest and influence in the same circle and with such men as are to compose such a Regiment; all in my Opinion entitle him to the favor of Congress, and lead me to believe, that in his promotion, the States will gain a good and valuable Officer for the sort of Troops he is particularly recommended to command."[2]

A few weeks later, however, the bulk of the rifle battalion was captured at Fort Washington and the issue of its command became mute.

So Morgan was appointed colonel of the 11th Virginia Regiment instead. He was joined by many of his men from the Quebec expedition, including Christian Febiger and William Heth, who were appointed Lieutenant Colonel and Major of the regiment, respectively.

In recognition of their conduct at Quebec, Peter Bruin and Charles Porterfield earned appointments as company captains in the regiment. This was contingent, however, on each of

---

[2] General Washington to John Hancock, 28 September, 1776 in *The Papers of George Washington, Vol. 6,* 421

them recruiting twenty-eight men into their respective companies.[3] Captain Bruin reached this goal in December. It took Captain Porterfield a few more weeks, but he too recruited the necessary men for his captain's commission.[4]

On February 3, 1777 the Virginia State Council named the ten companies that comprised the 11th Virginia.[5] Regiments raised a year earlier in Virginia consisted of seven musket and three rifle companies. Five of the six new regiments were organized in similar fashion. The 11th Virginia was different, however. Half of the regiment (five of its ten companies) consisted of independent rifle companies raised in the state during the summer of 1776, months before the 11th Regiment was formed.[6] Unfortunately, four of these companies were captured at Ft. Washington in mid-November. Thus, they were part of the 11th Virginia in name only. Just one of the original five rifle companies actually joined the regiment. It was commanded by Captain William Blackwell of Fauquier County. Captain Blackwell's first lieutenant was twenty year old John Marshall, future Chief Justice of the Supreme Court.

The other half of the 11th Virginia consisted of a company from Prince William County (under Captain Charles Gallihue) and two companies each from Loudoun County (under Captains William Smith and William Johnson) and Frederick County (under Captains Peter Bruin and Charles Porterfield). Colonel Morgan also recruited some men who were placed in Captain Porterfield's company.[7] Two other companies were added to the regiment after it arrived in New Jersey. Captain

---

[3] Ibid. 182

[4] H.R. McIlwaine, ed. *Journals of the Council of the State of Virginia, Vol. 1*, (Richmond: Virginia State Library, 1931), 325 and E.M. Sanchez-Saavedra, *A Guide to Virginia Military Organizations in the American Revolution, 1774-1787*, (Westminster, MD: Willow Bend , 1978), 65

[5] McIlwaine, 321

[6] Ibid.

[7] W.T.R. Saffell, *Records of the Revolutionary War, 3rd Ed.*, (Baltimore: Charles Saffell, 1894), 260

James Calderwood's company of Pennsylvania riflemen and Captain Gabriel Long's Virginia riflemen were attached to the 11th Virginia in the spring of 1777, presumably as replacements for the four captured rifle companies.[8]

The abundance of riflemen in Morgan's regiment, along with his association with such men, contributed to the long held belief that the 11th Virginia was solely a rifle regiment. This appears to be inaccurate, however. Although Captains Blackwell, Porterfield, Bruin, Long, and Calderwood commanded rifle companies, the two Loudoun county companies and the Prince William company, were probably made up of musket-men.

There are a number of points that support this. First, the 11th Virginia was never referred to, in contemporary sources, as a rifle regiment. In fact, at least two pension applications from members of the 11th Virginia, refer to the unit as, "*Morgan's musket regiment.*" In 1818 Eden Clevenger, a former rifleman in Captain Porterfield's company, claimed that he served, "*in the 11th Virginia Regiment, generally called Col. Morgan's musket regiment.*"[9] His claim was supported by Thomas Stothard, who declared that, "*he went out with Eden Clevenger in the regiment of musket men in the same company and messed with him all the time of service.*"[10]

The fact that some of Morgan's men marched north unarmed, and were supplied with weapons (probably muskets) when they arrived in camp, also supports the view that there were musket-men in the 11th Virginia. Lastly, when a special rifle corps was actually formed, in June, 1777, most members of the 11th Virginia remained with the regiment. And many of the riflemen who stayed exchanged their rifles for muskets, per order of General Washington.[11]

---

[8] Ibid. 256, 268

[9] Eden Clevenger Pension Application, in *Virginia Revolutionary Pension Applications, Vol. 20*, ed. John Dorman, 9

[10] Ibid. 10

[11] See Hening, *Statutes at Large*, and General Orders on 13 June, 1777

So while the 11th Virginia did have a higher proportion of riflemen in its ranks (compared to other Virginia regiments) it was not solely a rifle regiment.

Recruitment for the five new companies occurred over the winter. Each company was authorized to raise sixty-eight men, but it is doubtful that they all reached that number. General Washington, desperate for reinforcements, urged the states to send men as quickly as possible, regardless of whether their units were complete or not.[12] The first company from the 11th Virginia to head north was Captain Blackwell's. It departed sometime in January, before it was even assigned to the regiment. The men immediately underwent inoculation for small pox upon their arrival in Philadelphia.

General Washington had quietly begun inoculating the army in early February. On February 6th, he explained his decision to William Shippen, the future Director General of Military Hospitals for the Continental Army.

"Finding the Small pox to be spreading much and fearing that no precaution can prevent it from running through the whole of our Army, I have determined that the troops shall be inoculated...I have directed Doctr Bond to prepare immediately for inoculating in this Quarter, keeping the matter as secret as possible, and request that you will, without delay, inoculate All the Continental Troops that are in Philadelphia and those that shall come in as fast as they arrive." [13]

Note: The author contends that, until definitive evidence is produced to support claims that the 11th Virginia was raised solely as a rifle regiment, it is best to conclude that the 11th Virginia, like the other Virginia regiments, was a mixed unit, albeit with a higher proportion of riflemen than the other regiments.

[12] General Washington to Colonel George Weedon, 9 January, 1777 in *Writings of George Washington, Vo. 6*, (Washington, D.C.: U.S. Govt. Printing Office, 1932), 482

[13] General Washington to William Shippen Jr., 6 February, 1777 in *The Papers of George Washington, Vol. 8*, 264

Although the inoculations would better prepare the American army for the upcoming campaign, their immediate impact was to decrease the number of troops available to General Washington. As a result, he repeated his appeal to the states for more men.

On February 4th, 1777 the Virginia State Council, responding to General Washington's pleas, ordered Colonel Morgan to, "...*forthwith march to Head Quarters, to join the Army under the Command of His Excellency, General Washington.*"[14] Colonel Morgan and his officers, however, found recruiting in the second year of the war much harder than at the outbreak. When the order arrived, Morgan had few troops to send. It took three weeks for the 11th Virginia to partially comply with the Council's order. On February 23, 1777 Lieutenant Colonel Christian Febiger led three companies northward. Colonel Febiger announced his arrival in Philadelphia in a letter to Washington on March 6th.

> "...*I have the honor of informing your Excellency of my Arrival in this City with the first Company of our Regiment, two Companies more being on their March and hourly expected, those men, who are in Town are under Inoculation and recovering fast, as soon as they can be cloathed and arm'd, I shall march them to Camp.*"[15]

The shortage of clothing was, in part, the result of the small pox inoculation the men underwent. The process, which typically took a few weeks, required the men's old clothes be thoroughly washed and smoked before they left camp.[16] Of

---

[14] McIlwaine, 324

[15] Lt. Col. Christian Febiger to General Washington, 6 March 1777 in *The Papers of George Washington, Vol. 8,* 520

[16] General Washington to Major General Horatio Gates, 28 January, 1777 in *The Papers of George Washington, Vol. 8,* 172

course, General Washington preferred that new clothing be issued to the men, but there simply wasn't enough to go around.

In his letter, Colonel Febiger also suggested a few replacement companies for the ones that were lost at Fort Washington.

> *"Unfortunately the Government of Virginia have appointed to serve under us the 5 Companies, that formerly belonged to Col. Rawlin's Battalion, of which only one Commanded by Capt. Wm. Blackwell now in this City is existing, Capt. Sheppards, Wests, & Longs being chiefly taken at Fort Washington, and Capt. Brady is gone to Berkely on what Business or for what Purpose I know not. There are two Captains...John Paul Schott and James Calderwood, who both are very desirous of serving in our Regiment, and have desir'd me to request the Favour of your Excellency to permit them to join us in Room of two of those Companies that are taken."[17]*

Febiger concluded with a report on the five new companies of the regiment.

> *"Of the 5 new Companies allotted to us by the Government of Virginia, Capt. Bruin of Frederick and Gallihue of Prince William are hourly expected with full Companies, having been some Time on their March. Captains Wm. Johnson and Smith of Loudon will come in a Short Time under the Major and Colonel Morgan will come with the last whom I don't know, as it was not determin'd whether we should*

---

[17] Lt. Col. Febiger to General Washington, 6 March 1777, in *The Papers of George Washington, Vol. 8*, 520-521

have the Forquair or Dunmore Company, when I left Winchester."[18]

It appears that the last company to march north was actually Captain Charles Porterfield's. William Berkley, a private in Porterfield's company, recalled years later that he, "*...marched to Winchester, Va., in March 1777 where the troops rendezvoused and about 25 March were marched to Philadelphia and there inoculated for the small pox.*"[19] Humphrey Becket, another soldier in Captain Porterfield's company, recalled in his pension application that they joined the main army in New Jersey in April, 1777.[20]

The 11th Virginia in New Jersey

By mid April, the bulk of the 11th Virginia, numbering less than half its authorized strength, was posted near Bound Brook, New Jersey.[21] A month later, a troop return of all twelve Virginia regiments at Morristown, listed the 11th Virginia with only 185 privates fit for duty. Five of the regiment's captains were also recorded as present.[22] While it is unclear who the five were, Captain Porterfield's signature

---

[18] Ibid.
[19] William Berkley Pension Application, in *Virginia Revolutionary Pension Applications, Vol. 6,* ed. John Dorman, 60
[20] Humphrey Becket Pension Application, in *Virginia Revolutionary Pension Applications, Vol.9,* ed. John Dorman, 9
[21] A Return of the Troops...Under Command of Maj. Gen. Lincoln, May 3, 1777, Benjamin Lincoln Papers, Massachusetts Historical Society in Charles H. Lesser, ed. *The Sinews of Independence: Monthly Strength Reports of the Continental Army,* (Chicago: The University of Chicago Press, 1976), 45
[22] Report on Virginia Battalions, 17 May, 1777 in *George Washington Papers at the Library of Congress, 1741-1799: Series 4,* Image 943 (Online)

on a company payroll that month, (May), strongly suggests that he was one of them.

The payroll listed four sergeants, two corporals, one fifer, one cadet, and forty-five rank and file in Porterfield's company. An additional sheet listed two more corporals and eighteen riflemen. These were either remnants of the captured rifle companies at Fort Washington, or men who Colonel Morgan personally recruited. Regardless of their original status, they were now attached to Porterfield's company, and their addition brought his unit to full strength. Unfortunately, twenty-one men were sick and either in the hospital, or in Philadelphia recuperating.[23]

With the approach of summer, large numbers of recruits finally arrived. By mid May, the army's total strength topped 8,000 men, double the number for March.[24] The expectation was that by June, the number of men would exceed 12,000.[25]

In response to the influx of soldiers, General Washington re-organized the army. The 11th Virginia was brigaded with the 3rd, 7th, and 15th Virginia Regiments.[26] The 3rd Regiment was the most experienced of all of Virginia's continental units. It fought at Gwynn's Island, Harlem Heights, White Plains, Trenton, and Princeton. By contrast, the 7th Virginia, like the 11th regiment, had only recently arrived, and the 15th Virginia was due in camp shortly.

General William Woodford, of Caroline County, commanded the new brigade, which was placed in General

---

[23] Pay Roll for Capt. Charles Porterfield's Company of the Eleventh Virginia Regt. Commanded by Col. Daniel Morgan for the Month of May, 1777 in the Manuscript Collection, VA Hist. Society, Rec. No.: 132210

[24] Washington to Congress, 21 May, 1777 in *George Washington Papers at the Library of Congress 1741-1799: Series 3a Varick Transcripts, Letterbook 2*, Image 272 (Online)

[25] David Griffith to Major Levin Powell, 28 May, 1777 in Robert Powell's *Biographical Sketch of Col. Levin Powell, 1731-1810*, (Alexandria, Virginia: G.H. Ramey & Son, 1877), 77

[26] General Orders, 22 May, 1777, in *The Papers of George Washington*, Vol. 9, 495

Adam Steven's Division. Woodford originally commanded the 2nd Virginia regiment and was victorious at the battle of Great Bridge. Frustration at being passed over for promotion caused him to resign his commission in September, 1776. When Congress offered him a promotion, and command of a brigade, however, Woodford agreed to return.

Although the growth of the American army improved its capabilities and morale, General Washington declined to leave his fortified lines and meet the enemy in the open. At the same time, General Howe refused to attack the strong position of the Americans. Instead, he tried to lure them out of their earthworks. Washington refused to be drawn out, however, and a stalemate ensued for most of June.

Colonel Morgan used this period of inactivity to improve his regiment. He issued frequent orders to practice the manual of arms and the evolutions (marching). Morgan also stressed the need to keep the camp, arms, and men, as clean as possible.[27]

Colonel Morgan's direct involvement with the 11th Virginia was short lived, however. His experience, leadership, and reputation, made him the perfect choice to command a new corps of riflemen that General Washington created for the upcoming campaign.

---

[27] Orderly Book of Major William Heth of the Third (sic) Virginia Regiment, May 15 – July 1, 1777 in *Virginia Historical Society Collections, New Series, 11* (1892)
Accessed via the website: RevWar75.com
Note: The author contends that this orderly book has long been misidentified as belonging to the 3rd Virginia Regiment when in fact, it pertains to the 11th Virginia Regiment

Morgan's Rifle Corps

The formation of this rifle corps began on June 1st, when General Washington called for a count of all the riflemen in the army.

> *"The commanding officer of every Corps,"* ordered Washington, *"[is] to make a report early tomorrow morning...of the number of Rifle-men under his command...to include none but such as are known to be perfectly skilled in the use of these guns, and who are known to be active and orderly in their behavior."*[28]

Five hundred marksmen, chosen from this list, comprised Morgan's new unit.

On June 13th, General Washington informed Colonel Morgan of his appointment to command the rifle corps. He also outlined his expectations.

> *"The corps of Rangers newly formed, and under your command, are to be considered as a body of Light infantry, and are to act as such for which reason they will be exempted from the common duties of the line...I have sent for spears, which I expect shortly to receive and deliver to you, as a defense against horse."*[29]

That same day General Washington ordered that,

---

[28] General Orders, 1 June, 1777, in *The Papers of George Washington, Vol. 9,* 578

[29] General Washington to Colonel Daniel Morgan, 13 June, 1777, in *The Papers of George Washington, Vol. 10,* 31

"Such rifles as belong to the States...to be immediately exchanged with Col. Morgan for musquets...If a sufficient number of rifles (public property) can not be procured, the Brigadiers are requested to assist Col. Morgan, either by exchanging, or purchasing those that are private property."[30]

The 11th Virginia contributed a large number of men to Morgan's Rifle Corps. They spent the next two months serving as the eyes of the American army, participating in numerous scouting missions and skirmishes. In mid August, Morgan's Corps was ordered to join General Horatio Gates in New York. It was there, on the battlefield of Saratoga, that the riflemen distinguished themselves in battle.

While Colonel Morgan, and his riflemen, earned laurels through their participation in the Rifle Corps, the bulk of the 11th Virginia, including Captain Porterfield, remained with General Washington's army. Lieutenant Colonel Christian Febiger assumed temporary command of the regiment. He continued Colonel Morgan's practice of discipline and drill. Occasionally, large scale exercises, called Field Days, were held. These involved brigade size military maneuvers and included practice firings with blank cartridges.[31]

The 11th Virginia also participated in picquet duty. In late June, Captain William Blackwell's company guarded a mountain pass with Captain John Chilton's company from the 3rd Virginia. Chilton described the duty in a letter to his brother.

I am at this time stationed with 30 men to guard this pass; came here last night. Mr. Blackwell's & my

---

[30] General Orders, 13 June, 1777, in *The Papers of George Washington, Vol. 10,* 20
[31] Orderly Book of Major William Heth, June 13, 1777

*Company with me, except a few who stay in camp
with the baggage, we are all hearty, few complaints
being now in the Army of sickness, there is a small
lax but it wears off quickly. Our station is a pretty
agreeable one, only two miles from Camp where we
can at any time run for any necessary that we want
from that quarter. Then we have the advantage of
getting milk, butter &c. which are scarce articles in
Camp.*[32]

Tour of the Jerseys

In early July, General Washington received reports that a
large British force had boarded ships in New York. Their
destination puzzled and concerned Washington. Conventional
wisdom suggested that the British would sail up the Hudson
River to join General John Burgoyne's army. Burgoyne was
marching south, from Canada, with 7,000 men, in an effort to
split New England from the rest of the states.

Reports from New York, however, suggested that the fleet
was actually heading south. General Washington had to
consider that Philadelphia, via the Delaware River or
Chesapeake Bay, was Howe's destination. Or perhaps the
British were heading to Virginia or South Carolina. On the
other hand, a movement south might only be a ploy to draw
the American army in that direction, while Howe doubled
back and sailed up the Hudson River. General Washington
was simply unsure of Howe's intentions. As a result, he kept
the army in New Jersey, waiting for more definitive
intelligence.

In mid July, such intelligence falsely indicated that the
Hudson River was Howe's destination. In response, General
Washington led his army northward. They arrived in Chester,

---

[32] John Chilton to his Brother, 29 June, 1777 in *Tyler's Quarterly
Historical and Geneological Magazine, 10* (July 1930), 91

New York on July 23rd, only to turn around and march south two days later.[33]   The reason for the sudden change in direction was a report that Howe's fleet was spotted off of New Jersey, heading south.   The American army was dangerously out of position. Washington rushed his army southward, towards Philadelphia, covering seventy miles in three days.[34] Many men fell out of the march, straggling into camp hours after the army halted. Captain John Chilton, of the 3rd Virginia, described the march in his diary.

> "...we were ordered to sit down, in the Sun no water near, to refresh ourselves no victuals to eat as the (march) of last night was so late that nothing could be cooked, no wagons allowed to carry our Cooking utensils, the soldiers were obliged to carry their Kettles, pans, &c. in their hands, Clothes and provisions on their backs...As our march was a forced one & the Season extremely warm, the victuals became putrid with sweat & heat -- the Men badly off for Shoes, many being entirely barefoot."[35]

By August, Washington's army was camped only a day's march from Philadelphia. They remained there for most of the month, waiting for the British fleet, (which had once again disappeared over the eastern horizon), to reappear. Captain Porterfield and his men undoubtedly enjoyed the opportunity to rest a bit.   This respite ended on August 23rd, however, when the British fleet was spotted in the Chesapeake Bay. These reports convinced General Washington that the enemy was trying to approach Philadelphia from the south.   He immediately prepared the army to march. Hoping to impress the inhabitants of Philadelphia, General Washington ordered,

---

[33] Chilton Diary, 12-23 July, 1777 in *Tyler's Quarterly,* 284
[34] Ibid.
[35] Chilton Diary, 27 July, 1777 in *Tyler's Quarterly,* 286

"every Man to have clean clothes ready for the Morning, the Arms to be Furbished & bright."[36]

The next day, with sprigs of green in their hats and polished muskets in their hands, the army marched through the city. John Adams described the procession to his wife, Abigail.

"we have an army well appointed between us and Mr. Howe...so that I feel as secure here as if I was at Braintree." [37]

He also noted, however, that,

"our soldiers have not yet quite the air of soldiers. They don't step exactly in time. They don't hold up their heads quite erect, nor turn out their toes so exactly as they ought..."[38]

Nevertheless, these were the men charged with defending Philadelphia and the country. Onward they marched, towards the enemy, who, after a long and draining voyage, finally disembarked near Head of Elk, Maryland.[39]

---

[36] General Orders for 24 August, 1777 *The Papers of George Washington, Vol. 11,* 55

[37] Henry Ward, *Duty, Honor, or Country: General George Weedon and the American Revolution,* (Philadelphia: American Philosophical Society, 1979), 96-97

[38] Ibid.

[39] Chilton Diary, 25 August, 1777 in *Tyler's Quarterly,* 287

Chapter Four

Brandywine

With the British only a few miles away, General Washington prepared his army for battle. He formed a corps of light infantry, comprised of men from each brigade.[1] This seven hundred man detachment acted as an advance guard, or early warning system. Washington instructed General William Maxwell, the light corps commander, to keep a close eye on the enemy.

"I wish you very much to have the situation of the Enemy critically reconnoitered, to know as exactly as possible how and where they lie, in what places they are approachable; where their several guards are stationed, and the strength of them; and everything necessary to be known to enable us to judge, with precision, whether any advantage may be taken of their present divided state. No pains should be omitted to gain as much certainty, as can be had, in all these particulars."[2]

The 11th Virginia contributed a number of men to the light corps, including Lieutenant Colonel William Heth, Lieutenant John Marshall, and Captain Charles Porterfield. Porterfield was placed in command of an infantry company.

---

[1] General Orders, 28 August, 1777, in *The Papers of George Washington, Vol. 11*, 82

[2] General Washington to General William Maxwell, 3 September, 1777, in *The Papers of George Washington, Vol. 11*, 140

The Battle of Cooches Bridge

Two days after its formation, the light corps was ordered to the vicinity of Cooches Bridge. General Washington expected the British to advance via this route, and he wanted General Maxwell's detachment to harass and annoy the enemy as much as possible. Washington told General Maxwell that his men, *"should...lie quiet and still, and ought to be posted early tonight, as the Enemy will most probably move...between two and three O'clock."*[3]

It was another three days before the British marched, however. An advance guard, consisting of German jaegers British light infantry, and provincial dragoons, led the army. They set out from Aikin's Tavern at daybreak, on September 3rd, and, just as Washington predicted, headed for Cooches Bridge.

The route to the bridge was ideally situated for the type of fighting General Maxwell desired. Aware that his detachment was greatly outnumbered, Maxwell had no intention of facing the enemy in open combat. Instead, he hoped to delay their march with a series of ambushes. His men were instructed to strike the enemy from concealed positions, and when pressed, to fall back, reform, and hit them again. Thus, every tree, thicket, and rock along the road was a possible firing position for the Americans. British Captain John Montresor ominously described the terrain in his journal. *"...the Country is close-- the woods within shot of the road, frequently in front and flank and in projecting points towards the Road."*[4]

Captain Johann Ewald, with six dragoons, rode ahead of the British advance corps. They cautiously approached Maxwell's position around 9:00 a.m. Suddenly, shots rang out

---

[3] Ibid. 95

[4] "Journal of Captain John Montresor," 3 September, 1777, in *The Pennsylvania Magazine of History and Biography Vol. 5,* (Philadelphia: The Historical Society of Pennsylvania, 1881), 412

from the nearby wood, catching Ewald, and the dragoons, by surprise.

> *"I...had not gone a hundred paces from the advance guard,"* recalled Captain Ewald, *"when I received fire from a hedge, through which these six men* [the dragoons] *were all either killed or wounded. My horse, which normally was well used to fire, reared so high several times that I expected it would throw me. I cried out, "Foot jagers forward!" and advanced with them to the area from which the fire was coming...At this moment I ran into another enemy party with which I became heavily engaged. Lieutenant Colonel von Wurmb, who came with the entire Corps assisted by the light infantry, ordered the advance guard to be supported."* [5]

Maxwell's men, according to plan, fell back. *"A Continued Smart irregular fire* [ensued] *for near two miles,"* reported Captain Montresor.[6] Sergeant Thomas Sullivan, of the British 49th Regiment, attributed the, "hot fire" of the Americans to their strong position.[7]

The engagement lasted into the afternoon, with Captain Porterfield and the light corps fighting from tree to tree. Gradually they withdrew to Iron Hill and Cooches Bridge. As the British pressed forward, they saw American troops scurrying in the woods on Iron Hill.[8] General Howe ordered

---

[5] Captain Johann Ewald, *Diary of the American War: A Hessian Journal,* trans. & ed. By Joseph Tustin, (New Haven: Yale Univ. Press, 1979), 77
[6] Montressor Journal, 412
[7] "Before and After the Battle of Brandywine: Extracts from the Journal of Sergeant Thomas Sullivan of H.M. Forty-Ninth Regiment of Foot", 3 September, 1777 in *The Pennsylvania Magazine of History and Biography, Vol. 31,* (Philadelphia: Historical Society of Pennsylvania, 1907), 410
[8] Ewald, 78

the British advance guard to drive the enemy off. Captain Ewald led the way and recalled that,

> "*The charge was sounded, and the enemy was attacked so severely and with such spirit by the jagers that we became masters of the mountain after a seven hour engagement.*"[9]

Ewald described the fighting as intense.

> "*The majority of the jagers came to close quarters with the enemy, and the hunting sword was used as much as the rifle.*"[10]

The British also used artillery in the attack, but with little effect. One of the biggest threats to the Americans occurred when Lieutenant Colonel Robert Abercromby led a battalion of British light infantry across Christianna Creek, and around the left flank of Maxwell's corps. Abercromby hoped to cut off Maxwell's route of retreat. Fortunately for the Americans, Abercromby's battalion stumbled upon an impassable swamp and was unable to complete the encirclement.

It is unclear whether the Americans were even aware of this threat to their rear. They had their hands full with the jaegers, who steadily pushed Maxwell's men off Iron Hill and towards Cooches Bridge. "*The jagers alone enjoyed the honor of driving the enemy out of his advantageous position,*" boasted Ewald years later[11]

Although Maxwell's men were forced from Iron Hill, they still had some fight left in them. Sergeant Sullivan observed that,

---

[9] Ibid.

[10] Ibid.

[11] Ibid.

"...after a hot fire the enemy retreated towards their main body, by Iron Hill. They made a stand at the Bridge for some time, but the pursuing Corps made them quit that post also, and retire with loss."[12]

General Maxwell eventually withdrew from Cooches Bridge and rejoined the main army. Despite their retreat, Captain Porterfield, and the rest of Maxwell's Corps, had performed their mission admirably. They harassed the enemy and delayed their advance to the point that General Howe halted his army for the rest of the day.[13]

General Washington, pleased with the conduct of the light corps, wrote to Congress, speculating that Maxwell's detachment inflicted considerable damage on the enemy.

"This morning," he wrote, *"the Enemy came out with considerable force and three pieces of Artillery, against our Light advanced Corps, and after some pretty smart skirmishing obliged them to retreat, being far inferior in number and without Cannon. The loss on either side is not yet ascertained. Our's, tho not exactly known, is not very considerable; Theirs, we have reason to believe, was much greater, as some of our parties composed of expert Marksmen, had Opportunities of giving them several, close, well directed Fires, more particularly in One instant, when a body of Riflemen formed a kind of Ambuscade."*[14]

---

[12] Sullivan Journal, 410

[13] Montressor Journal, 413

[14] General Washington to John Hancock, 3 September 1777, in *The Papers of George Washington, Vol. 11*, 135

Although General Washington was confident that the Americans got the best of the British, accurate casualty figures are difficult to determine. Both sides claimed they inflicted more loss on the enemy than they sustained. It appears, however, that the losses were rather insignificant, ranging between twenty- five to fifty men each.[15]

Maxwell's Corps re-joined the American army at Red Clay Creek after the battle. They took up new positions in advance of the army and were ordered to maintain a close watch on the enemy.[16] Two days after the skirmish, General Washington, anxious about the enemy's lack of activity, sent General Maxwell the following instructions.

> "*I should be glad to hear how the Enemy are situated and what they seem to be about. Send out reconnoitering parties under good intelligent officers to inspect the different parts of their Camp, and gain as exact an insight as possible into their circumstances...You should always have small advanced parties towards the Enemy's lines, about the hour of the morning you expect them to move, as it is of essential importance to us, to have the earliest intelligence of it.*"[17]

---

[15] General Howe reported losses of 3 dead and 21 wounded. Sergeant Thomas Sullivan reported identical numbers in his journal. Captain Ewald, however, claimed losses of 11 dead and 45 wounded. The reports of American losses also vary. Captain Montresor claimed that, "*the rebels left about 20 dead*". Major Baurmeister put that number at 30. Captain Muenchhausen claimed 41 rebels were buried by the British, including five officers. For his part, General Washington reported to Congress that, "*...we had forty killed and wounded, and as our own Men were thinly posted they must have done more damage upon a close Body then they received.*"

[16] Reed, 89

[17] General Washington to General William Maxwell, 5 September, 1777 in *The Papers of George Washington Vol. 11*, 154

Captain Porterfield was undoubtedly one of the "good, intelligent officers" sent to reconnoiter the enemy's camp. There was little to report, however, as the British remained inactive.

The situation changed on September 7th. Reports reached General Washington that the enemy had stripped itself of its excess baggage in preparation for a march. General Washington responded with similar orders.

"The General has received a confirmation...that the enemy have disencumbered themselves of all their baggage, even to their tents, reserving only their blankets and such part of the cloathing as is absolutely necessary. This indicates a speedy & rapid movement, and points out the necessity of following the example, and ridding ourselves for a few days of every thing we can possibly dispense with...Officers should only retain their blankets, great coats, and three or four shirts of under cloaths, and the men should, besides what they have on, keep only a Blanket, and a shirt a piece, and such as have it, a great coat – All trunks, chests, boxes, other bedding, and cloathes... [are] to be sent away, 'till the elapsing of a few days shall determine whether the enemy mean an immediate attack, or not."[18]

Another day passed before General Howe's intentions became clear. Rather than confront the Americans in a costly frontal assault, General Howe marched his army north, in an attempt to gain the right flank of the Americans.

Determined to protect both his flank, and Philadelphia, General Washington responded by rushing his army northward. His destination was Chadd's Ford, the likely

---

[18] General Orders for 7 September, 1777 in *The Papers of George Washington, Vol. 11*, 167-168

British crossing point over Brandywine Creek. The Americans marched with urgency and arrived at the ford on September 9th.

Advance elements of General Howe's army, which had a longer route to march, arrived at Kennett Square, several miles west of Chadd's Ford, that same evening. General Howe, with the main portion of his army, arrived the next morning. He remained at Kennett Square on September 10th, consolidating his force and devising a plan of attack. The stage was set for a major clash.

Battle of Brandywine

With only a few miles separating the two armies, General Washington once again turned to Maxwell's light infantry corps to act as his eyes and ears. Augmented by the addition of local militia, the corps numbered around 800 men.[19] It was sent across the Brandywine to screen the army and reconnoiter the approaches to Chadd's Ford.[20] General Maxwell positioned a large portion of his men, as well as a few light cannon, on a ridge overlooking the west bank of the Brandywine and the road leading to the ford.[21] He placed smaller detachments further out, towards the enemy.

General Light Horse Harry Lee, commenting on the battle, in his memoirs, wrote that,

"Three small detachments, commanded by Lieutenant Colonels Parker, Heth, and Simms, of the Virginia line, were early in the morning posted by the brigadier [Maxwell] contiguous to the road, some distance in his front; and Captain Porterfield, with a

---

[19] Samuel Smith, *The Battle of Brandywine*, (Monmouth Beach, NJ: Philip Freneau Press, 1976), 9
[20] Reed, 113
[21] Smith, 10

company of infantry, preceded these parties with orders to deliver his fire as soon as he should meet the van of the enemy, and then fall back. "[22]

Horse patrols extended almost to Kennett Square with orders to sound the alarm when the enemy approached.

The British commenced their march towards the Americans at daybreak, on September 11th, 1777.[23] They marched in two separate columns along two separate roads.[24] General Howe, with over 8,000 men, headed north, on a seventeen mile trek that, he hoped, would place him on the right flank of the American army.[25] General Knyphausen, with just under 7,000 men, marched east, straight towards the American army at Chadd's Ford.[26] His column was a decoy, or holding force. General Howe hoped to duplicate his success at Long Island by feigning a frontal attack, and striking the Americans on their vulnerable flank. Timing and deception were key elements of the plan. General Knyphausen had to convince the Americans that his force was the main assault. First, however, Knyphausen had to deal with General Maxwell's light infantry.

Knyphausen's advance guard consisted of the Queen's Rangers, (350 men), Captain Patrick Ferguson's Rifle Corps, (130 men), and a small detachment of cavalry.[27] Ferguson's men carried a novelty to war, breech loading rifles. These

---

[22] Henry Lee, *The Revolutionary War Memoirs of General Henry Lee, ed. by Robert E. Lee,* (New York: Da Capo Press, 1998, Originally published in 1812 as, *Memoirs of the War in the Southern Department of the United States*), 89

[23] Sullivan Journal, 412

[24] " Letters of Major Baurmeister During the Philadelphia Campaign," in *The Pennsylvania Magazine of History and Biography, Vol. 59* eds. Bernard Uhlendorf and Edna Vosper, (Philadelphia: Historical Society of Pennsylvania, 1935), 404

[25] Smith, 9

[26] Ibid.

[27] Ibid. 10

59

weapons, developed by Captain Ferguson himself, allowed for faster and more accurate fire. They had yet to be used in battle, however, and Ferguson was eager to demonstrate their usefulnes.[28]

Knyphausen's vanguard encountered the enemy less than a mile into their march. A few American light horsemen, refreshing themselves at Welch's Tavern, were startled to see an enemy column advancing toward them.[29] The Americans scurried out the back door, escaping injury and capture. Their horses, however, did not fair so well, and were pressed into British service.[30]

The first deadly encounter occurred soon afterwards. As the British approached Kennett Meetinghouse, they were suddenly attacked by Captain Charles Porterfield's company. Lieutenant Colonel William Heth, in a letter to Colonel Daniel Morgan, described the incident.

> "...our valuable Friend Porterfield began the action with day light – he killed (himself) the first man who fell that day – His conduct through the whole day – was such, as has acquired him the greatest Honor – A great proportion of British Officers fell by a party under his command & Capt. Waggoners (who is a brave officer) and I find it impossible to conceal my pride, from having in possession an Elegant double gilted mounted small sword – a Trophy of their success."[31]

---

[28] Ibid.

[29] Bruce E. Moway, *September 11, 1777: Washington's Defeat at Brandywine Dooms Philadelphia*, (PA: White Mane Books, 2002), 84

[30] Ibid.

[31] Heth to Morgan, 2 October 1777 in "The Diary of Lieutenant William Heth while a Prisoner in Quebec, 1776", edited by B. Floyd Flickinger, *Annual Papers of the Winchester Historical Society*, (Winchester: The Society, 1931), 33

Battle of Brandywine: Morning Phase

Despite the shock of the ambush, the British rapidly advanced and forced Captain Porterfield to withdraw to the next American position. Henry Lee wrote that,

> *"The British van pressed forward rapidly and incautiously, until it lined the front of the detachment commanded by Lt. Col. Simms, who poured in a close and destructive fire, and then retreated to the light corps."* [32]

While it is difficult to determine with certainty, Sergeant Thomas Sullivan of Britain's 49th Regiment may have described this encounter from a different perspective.

> *"The Queen's Rangers and Rifle Corps..."* wrote Sullivan, *"advancing to the foot of a hill, saw the enemy formed behind the fence,* [and] *were deceived by the Rebel's telling them, that they would deliver up their arms; but upon advancing they fired a volley upon our men, and took to their heels, killed and wounded about thirty of the Corps."* [33]

Although this second ambush staggered Knyphausen's advance corps, they pressed forward, meeting steady resistance all the way.

> *"...the enemys Light infantry and Riflemen,"* noted Sergeant Sullivan, *"kept up a running fire, mixed with regular vollies, for 5 miles."* [34]

Major Carl Baurmeister, who was with General Knyphausen, confirmed the duration of the fight. *"The skirmishing*

---

[32] Lee, 89
[33] Sullivan Journal, 413
[34] Ibid.

continued to the last hills of Chadd's Ford," wrote Baurmeister, after the battle.[35]

As Knyphausen's advance guard neared the Brandywine, they descended a long hill, and approached a portion of the road that passed through marshy land. Woods and hills bordered the road, providing plenty of cover for Maxwell's troops.[36] *"Heretofore the enemy had been repulsed by our vanguard alone,"* wrote Baurmeister, *"but now the engagement became more serious..."*[37]

General Knyphausen sent a brigade forward to re-enforce his depleted advance corps. Artillery was also placed on a nearby hill and commenced firing at the Americans in the woods and behind some hastily built breastworks on the opposite hill.

> *"We played upon them with two 6 pounders for half an hour,"* recalled Sergeant Sullivan, *"and drove them out of the breastworks, which was made of loose wood upon the declivity of the hill.[38]*

Major Baurmeister gave a more detailed account of this part of the battle. While the artillery bombarded Maxwell's men,

> *"...the Queen's Rangers...proceeded to the left and after a short but very rapid musketry-fire, supported by the 23rd English Regiment...drove the rebels out of their woods and straight across the lowland. Under cover of a continuous cannonade, the 28th English Regiment went off to the right of the column, and soon the rebels, who had been shouting "Hurrah"*

---

[35] Baurmeister Letters, 405
[36] Ibid.
[37] Ibid.
[38] Sullivan Journal, 413

and firing briskly from a gorge in front of us, were quickly put to flight."[39]

Sergeant Sullivan, positioned near the center of the attack, recounted the final push that forced Captain Porterfield and the rest of Maxwell's light corps across the Brandywine.

"As we crossed the brook [Ring Run] *they formed behind another fence at a field's distance, from whence we soon drove 'em, and a Battalion of Hessians, which formed at the left of our Brigade, fell in with them as they retreated...and after a smart pursuit...they* [the Americans] *crossed the Brandywine and took up post on that side; leaving a few men killed and a few more wounded behind."[40]*

It was only 10:30 in the morning when the last of Maxwell's men crossed the Brandywine and rejoined the American army.[41] They were tired from three hours of intense fighting. Surprisingly, however, according to Lieutenant Colonel Heth, American losses were, *"inconsiderable in comparison with the Enemys".[42]* General Washington's aide, Lieutenant Colonel Robert Harrison, concurred with Heth. In a letter to Congress, written that same day, Harrison summed up the morning's action.

"When I had the Honor of addressing you this morning, I mentioned that the Enemy were advancing and had began a Canonade; I would now beg leave to inform you, that they have kept up a brisk fire from their Artillery ever since. Their advanced party was

---

[39] Baurmeister Letters, 405
[40] Sullivan Journal, 413-414
[41] Baurmeister Letters, 406
[42] William Heth to Col. Daniel Morgan, 30 September, 1777 in *"The Diary of Lieutenant William Heth while a Prisoner in Quebec, 1777,* 31

attacked by our light Troops under Genl Maxwell, who crossed the Brandywine for that purpose and had posted his Men on some high Grounds on each side of the Road. The fire from our people was not of long duration as the Enemy pressed on in force, but was very severe. What loss the Enemy sustained cannot be ascertained with precision, but from our situation and briskness of the Attack, it is the general opinion, particularly of those, who were engaged, that they had at least Three Hundred Men killed & wounded. Our damage is not exactly known, but from the best Accounts we have been able to obtain, It does not exceed fifty in the whole.[43]

While it is probable that Harrison's estimate of enemy losses was exaggerated, it is also likely, given the nature of the fight, that Knyphayusen's men sustained much higher casualties than the Americans.

For the next six hours each side remained relatively still. Knyphausen's detachment waited for General Howe's signal to attack, and the Americans waited for Knyphausen to cross the Brandywine. During this pause, General Knyphausen took measures to convince Washington that an attack was indeed imminent.

"The column under Lieut. General Knyphausen," wrote Sergeant Sullivan of the 49th Regiment, *"as had been previously conserted, kept the enemy amused in the course of the day, with cannon, and the appearance of forcing the Ford, without intending to pass it, until the attack upon the enemy's right should take place."*[44]

---

[43] Lieutenant Colonel Robert Harrison to Congress, 11 September, 1777 in *The Papers of George Washington Vol. 11,* 199

[44] Sullivan Journal, 416

Lieutenant John Marshall, who served in Maxwell's Corps, witnessed Knyphausen's demonstrations.

"Knyphausen...paraded on the heights, reconnoitred the American army, and appeared to be making dispositions to force the passage of the river."[45]

Marshall recounted that during this lull, small parties of Americans crossed the creek. Scattered firing occurred all day but to little effect.[46] One such incident, however, involving a party of men under Captains Porterfield and Waggoner, proved costly to the enemy. According to Marshall, who witnessed the incident, Captains Porterfield and Waggoner led a detachment across the creek that,

"engaged the British flank guard very closely, killed a captain with ten or fifteen privates, drove them from the wood, and were on the point of taking a field piece. The sharpness of the skirmish soon drew a large body of the British to that quarter, and the Americans were again driven over the Brandywine."[47]

Washington's aide, Lieutenant Colonel Harrison, may have described the same encounter in his letter to Congress.

"After the [morning] *Affair, the Enemy halted upon the Heights, where they have remained ever since...There has been a scattering loose fire between our parties on each side of the Creek since the Action in the Morning, which just now*

---

[45] John Marshall, *The Life of George Washington, Vol. 2,* (New York: William Wise & Co., 1925, originally published in 1838), 299

[46] Ibid.

[47] Ibid. 300

became warm when Genl Maxwell pushed over with his Corps, and drove them from their Ground with the loss of thirty Men left dead on the Spot, among 'em a Captn of the 49th, and a number of Intrenching Tools with which they were throwing up a Battery."[48]

It appears that Sergeant Thomas Sullivan also described the encounter, albeit with a much different interpretation of the action. He recorded in his diary that,

A company of the 28th and a company of our Regiment advanced upon the hill to the right of the Ford, and in front of the enemy's left flank, in order to divert them, who were posted at a hundred yards distance in their front, behind trees, to the amount of 500, all chosen marksmen. A smart fire maintained on both sides for two hours, without either parties quitting their posts. Out of the two companies there were about 20 men killed and wounded...and two 6 pounders were ordered up the hill to dislodge the enemy if possible...These guns played upon them for some time, but they were so concealed under cover of the trees, that it was to no purpose...The guns were ordered back and also the two companies in order to draw the enemy after them from the trees, which scheme had the desired effect, for they quitted their post and advanced to the top of the hill where they were attacked [by] four companies of the 10th Battalion, in front, while the 40th made a charge upon their left flank, by going round the hill, and put them to an immediate rout."[49]

---

[48] Lt. Col. Harrison to Congress, 11 September, 1777, *The Papers of George Washington, Vol. 11,* 199

[49] Sullivan Journal, 414

It is difficult to determine, with certainty, whether the three accounts are of the same incident. Nonetheless, it is clear that skirmishing continued near Chadd's Ford well into the afternoon, and Captain Charles Porterfield and his men were heavily involved.

At American headquarters, conflicting reports of enemy troop movements towards his right flank concerned General Washington. At first, when it appeared that the reports were accurate, Washington saw an opportunity to strike his divided enemy. He ordered Generals Sullivan and Greene to lead their divisions across the creek and attack. But then new reports arrived that denied any such flanking movement. If these reports were true, Sullivan and Greene risked confronting the entire British army. The situation was too uncertain, so Washington cancelled the attack.

By the early afternoon, however, it was clear that the British were indeed moving against the American right. Believing that it was too late to take the offensive, Washington ordered Generals Sullivan, Stirling, and Stephen, to change their division fronts (along Brandywine Creek) and re-deploy a few miles away, near the Birmingham Meeting House. General Stirling and Stephen arrived ahead of Sullivan's division, and immediately deployed on the hills southwest of the Meeting House. A mile to the north, thousands of enemy troops, prepared to attack.

Brigadier General William Woodford's brigade was placed on the right flank of the American line, about three hundred yards from the Meeting House. The men of the 7th, 11th and 15th Virginia regiments, including members of Captain Charles Porterfield's own company, prepared for battle. Woodford's position, on the extreme right of the American line, meant that his own right flank was uncovered. To protect it, he sent the 170 men of his most experienced regiment, the 3rd Virginia, to occupy an orchard a hundred yards north of the Meeting House. This placed them nearly 400 yards away from the American line. Colonel Thomas Marshall's men crossed a deep vale and took position in what became known as Marshall's Wood. General George Weedon wrote after the battle that the 3rd Virginia,

> "...had orders to hold the wood as long as it was tenable & then retreat to the right of the brigade."[50]

The 3rd Virginia's detached and exposed position became even more so when the entire American line shifted to the right to allow General Sullivan's division to position itself on the left. General Weedon noted that,

> "In making this Alteration, unfavorable Ground, made it necessary for Woodford to move his Brigade 200 Paces back of the Line & threw Marshall's wood in his front."[51]

The 3rd Virginia was now over 500 yards in front of its brigade. The men must have felt very isolated in this position, yet they held their post.

The battle began around 3:30 p.m. when the British advance guard, comprised of German jaegers, British dragoons, and light infantry, marched down Osborne Hill towards the orchard. As they neared present day Street Road, they, *"received the fire from about 200 men in an orchard."*[52] This unexpected resistance caused them to take cover behind a fence, two hundred paces from the 3rd Virginia.[53] Captain Johann Ewald, commanding the British advance force, described the encounter.

---

[50] Brigadier General George Weedon's Correspondence Account of the Battle of Brandywine, 11 September, 1777. The original manuscript letter is in the collections of the Chicago Historical Society, Transcribed by Bob McDonald, 2001
[51] Ibid.
[52] Smith, 16
[53] Ibid. 17

"About half past three I caught sight of some infantry and horsemen behind a village on a hill in the distance. I drew up at once and deployed...I reached the first houses of the village with the flankers of the jagers, and Lt. Hagen followed me with the horsemen. But unfortunately for us, the time this took favored the enemy and I received extremely heavy small-arms fire from the gardens and houses, through which, however, only two jaegers were wounded. Everyone ran back, and I formed them again behind the fences or walls at a distance of two hundred paces from the village... "[54]

The 3rd Virginia held its ground, and awaited the enemy's next move. When the main battle line of the British army arrived at the fence, they too momentarily halted. The 3rd Virginia's fire, along with the artillery of Woodford's brigade, was deadly and accurate. One British officer reported that,

"the trees [were] cracking over ones head. The branches riven by the artillery, the leaves falling as in autumn by the grapeshot. "[55]

---

[54] Ewald Journal, 84-85
[55] Smith, 17

Battle of Brandywine: Afternoon Phase

The British resumed the attack, however, and their overwhelming numbers pushed the 3rd Virginia out of the orchard. Colonel Marshall re-positioned his men about one hundred paces to the rear, behind a stone wall at the Birmingham Meeting House. The 3rd Virginia, sheltered by the wall, maintained such a heavy fire that the British veered around the flanks of the Virginians, rather than confront them head on. [56]

General Weedon, proud of his old regiment's conduct, noted that Colonel Marshall and his men,

> *"...received the Enemy with a Firmness which will do Honor to him & his little Corps, as long as the 11th of Sept. is remembered. He continued there ¾ of one Hour, & must have done amazing execution."*[57]

General Harry Lee concurred, writing in his memoirs that the 3rd Virginia,

> *"...bravely sustained itself against superior numbers, never yielding one inch of ground and expending thirty rounds a man, in forty-five minutes."*[58]

The 3rd Virginia could not hold its position indefinitely, however. With more than a quarter of its men out of action, and the enemy nearly surrounding them, the regiment had no choice but to withdraw.

Captain Charles Porterfield and the rest of Maxwell's light corps heard the fight at Birmingham. So did General Knyphausen. It was the signal to begin his attack. General Knyphausen commenced a "fearful cannonade" to soften up

---

[56] Ibid.
[57] Weedon Correspondence
[58] Lee, 89-90

the Americans and then sent his troops across the creek.[59] They crossed at Chadd's Ferry, (a few hundred yards below Chadd's Ford), because it was less obstructed and further away from an American battery (Colonel Thomas Proctor's) at Chadd's Ford.[60] This put them on a collision course with General Anthony Wayne's brigade of Pennsylvanians, who were posted on an elevation overlooking Chadd's Ferry. General Wayne had a small artillery battery of his own, and commenced firing on the enemy.[61]

According to Captain Ewald, Knyphausen's men,

> *"waded through the creek...which is about fifty paces wide and a half-man deep, under grapeshot and small-arms fire."*[62]

Sergeant Sullivan, who participated in the crossing, recorded that the 4th Battalion,

> *"...forded the River under a heavy fire of Musquetry...We were up to our middle in the river, and the rear line of the enemy being posted upon a hill on the other side of the road, played upon us with four pieces of cannon during that attack."*[63]

Knyphausen's aide, Major Carl Baurmeister, recalled that,

> *"The crossing was offered on our right wing, about 250 paces from the enemy's battery, [Proctor's] which lay a little to the left of the ford. After*

---

[59] Baurmeister Letter, 406
[60] Smith, 22
[61] Ibid. 23
[62] Ewald Journal, 82
[63] Sullivan Journal, 416-417

crossing, the troops attacked them furiously, partly with the bayonet."[64]

When they reached the other side, Knyphausen's men pressed forward. Sergeant Sullivan described the attack on General Wayne's brigade.

"...the enemy's cannon, [presumably Wayne's battery] missing fire in the Battery as they [4th Battalion] crossed, and before the gunners could fire them off, the men of that Battalion put them to the bayonet, and forced the enemy from the entrenchment, who drawing up in the field and orchard just by, rallied afresh and fought bayonet to bayonet, but the rest of the two Brigades, 71st and Rangers coming up, [obliged the Americans] to retreat in the greatest confusion, leaving their artillery and ammunition in the field."[65]

Captain Ewald described the capture of the main American battery, under Colonel Procter. Knyphausen's men,

...continued their march...in the best order without firing a shot, deployed with great composure, attacked the battery and the escort with the bayonet, stabbed down all who offered resistance, and captured four cannon and a howitzer."[66]

Captain Porterfield, and the rest of Maxwell's light corps, was positioned a bit to the rear of Chadd's Ford, on a hill overlooking the Chester Road.[67] This placed them away from

---

[64] Baurmeister Letters, 406-407
[65] Sullivan Journal, 416-417
[66] Ewald Journal, 82
[67] Smith, 23

the initial fighting. However, Knyphausen's force eventually started down the road, and Maxwell's corps, like the rest of the American left wing, became heavily engaged.[68]

To make matters worse, the far right section of General Howe's flank attack (at Birmingham) swung too far west and completely missed the fight there. However, their steady advance brought them to the right and rear of Maxwell's corps. The sudden appearance of the enemy sparked a general retreat of the entire American left wing.[69] Major Baurmeister recalled that,

> *"Our regiments gained one height after another as the enemy withdrew. They withstood one more rather severe attack behind some houses and ditches in front of their left wing. Finally, we saw the entire enemy line and four guns, which fired frequently, drawn up on another height in front of a dense forest, their right wing resting on the Chester road. By the time it grew dark, the van of the left column of General Howe had joined us...The enemy, however, gained the road to Chester in considerable confusion. Had not darkness favored their retreat, we might have come into possession of much artillery, munitions, and horses."[70]*

The situation on the American right wing, at Birmingham, was no better. The British forced the Americans off the heights and towards the village of Dillworth. General Nathaniel Greene's division, originally held in reserve at Chadd's Ford, rushed to their aid, covering four miles in forty-

---

[68] Ibid.
[69] Mowday, 147
[70] Baurmeister Letters, 407

five minutes.[71] Lieutenant James McMichael, described what happened when they arrived on the field.

"We took the front and attacked the enemy at 5:30 p.m., and being engaged with their grand army, we at first were obliged to retreat a few yards and formed in an open field when we fought without giving way on either side until dark. Our ammunition almost expended, firing ceased on both sides, when we received orders to proceed to Chester...This day for a severe and successive engagement exceeded all I ever saw. Our regiment fought at one stand about an hour under incessant fire, and yet the loss was less than at Long Island; neither were we so near each other as at Princeton, our common distance being about 50 yards."[72]

General Greene's stand near Dillworth helped the Americans conduct an orderly retreat. The day, however, clearly belonged to the British. They held the battlefield, and eleven American field pieces. Their 543 casualties were only half the American losses. [73] And their objective, Philadelphia, lay just a few miles away, defended by a weakened and presumably dispirited enemy.

Yet, although the Battle of Brandywine was another defeat for General Washington and his army, it was not as decisive as

---

[71] Ward,

[72] "Diary of Lieutenant James McMichael," *The Pennsylvania Magazine of History and Biography, Vol. 16*, (Philadelphia: Historical Society of Pennsylvania, 1892), 150

[73] Smith, 23

Determining an exact figure of American losses is difficult. Many of those listed as captured, were also listed as wounded, so there was a lot of double counting. The British claimed they buried almost 400 Americans. John Marshall put the number at 300 killed and 600 wounded, of which 300-400 were also captured. This number corresponds with Sergeant Sullivan's report of 300 killed, 600 wounded and 400 captured.

it appeared. In fact, some applauded the fact that the Americans fought as hard as they did. It was certainly a far cry from their conduct at Long Island and Kip's Bay.

In a midnight report to Congress, General Washington tried to soften the blow of another loss.

"I am sorry to inform you that in this days engagement we have been obliged to leave the enemy the masters of the field. Unfortunately the intelligence received of the enemys [movements] ...was uncertain & contradictory...This prevented my making a disposition adequate to the force with which the enemy attacked us on our right...yet our loss of men is not, I am persuaded, very considerable; I believe much less than the enemys."[76]

Two days later, in an effort to boost morale, General Washington issued the following order.

"The General, with peculiar satisfaction, thanks those gallant officers and soldiers, who, on the 11th instant, bravely fought in their country and its cause...Altho' the event of that day, from some unfortunate circumstances, was not so favorable as could be wished, the General has the satisfaction of assuring the troops, that from every account he has been able to obtain, the enemy's loss greatly exceeded ours...The Honorable Congress, in consideration of the gallant behaviour of the troops on Thursday last – their fatigue since – and from a full conviction that on every future occasion they will manifest a bravery worthy of the cause they have undertaken to defend – having been pleased to order

---

[76] General Washington to Congress, 11 September, 1777 in *The Papers of George Washington, Vol. 11,* 200

thirty hogsheads of rum to be distributed among them...the Commander in Chief...orders the Commissary General of Issues, to deliver to each officer and soldier, one gill per day, while it lasts."[77]

---

[77] General Orders for 13 September, 1777 in *The Papers of George Washington, Vol. 11,* 211-212

Chapter Five

Philadelphia to Valley Forge

The weeks following Brandywine were difficult for Charles Porterfield and the American army. Constant marching, often on muddy roads, wore the men down. The absence of most of the baggage and tents, which were sent to the rear before the battle, added to their suffering. Lieutenant John Marshall described the situation.

> *"The effect of these hardships was much increased by the privations under which the American troops suffered. While in almost continual motion, wading deep rivers, and encountering every vicissitude of the seasons, they were without tents, nearly without shoes or winter clothes, and often without food."*[1]

Maxwell's corps had the additional responsibility of serving as the rear guard of the army.[2] Fortunately, General Howe, as he was prone to do, delayed his pursuit. Thus, most of Maxwell's time was spent collecting stragglers from the American army.

General Washington, however, was determined to challenge the British army again. On September 15th he issued orders that emphasized his resolve.

> *"In future, whenever the men are formed for action, the Serjeants are to be placed in the ranks, on the flanks of subdivisions, that the benefit of their fire*

---

[1] Marshall, 312

[2] General Orders, 12 September, 1777 in *The Papers of George Washington, Vol. 11,* 204

may not be lost—The Brigadiers and Officers commanding regiments are also to post some good officers in the rear, to keep the men in order; and if in time of action, any man, who is not wounded, whether he has arms or not, turns his back upon the enemy, and attempts to run away, or to retreat before orders are given for it, those officers are instantly to put him to death – The man does not deserve to live, who basely flies, breaks his solemn engagements, and betrays his country."[3]

The American army regrouped under these orders and marched towards the enemy. Maxwell's corps was placed in the van. When the army halted for the evening, General Maxwell sent scouting parties to reconnoiter and secure the perimeter. He reported their findings to Washington the next morning.

"I have had a party of 50 Just come in from Turks head, at 12 oclock they found a party of the Enemys light Horse a little on this side but on the first discovery they made off...I have another party of 50 I expect in soon, there is a large party of Rifle Men gone out this Morning."[4]

The patrols revealed that General Howe's army was also on the move. Both sides once again prepared for battle, sending advance parties forward to skirmish. Before the armies were fully engaged, however, a torrential rain set in. Lieutenant John Marshall described the storm's impact.

---

[3] General Orders, 15 September, 1777 in *The Papers of George Washington, Vol. 11*, 233
[4] Brigadier General Maxwell to General Washington, 16 September, 1777 in *The Papers of George Washington, Vol. 11*, 249

"The advanced parties had met, and were beginning to skirmish, when they were separated by a heavy rain, which, becoming more and more violent, rendered the retreat of the Americans a measure of absolute necessity...The gun locks not being well secured, their muskets soon became unfit for use. Their cartridge-boxes had been so artificially constructed, as not to protect the ammunition from the tempest. Their cartridges were soon damaged; and this mischief was the more serious, because very many of the soldiers were without bayonets"[5]

General Washington gave a similar account of what was dubbed, the Battle of the Clouds. He informed Congress that,

"...the two Armies were upon the point of coming to a general Engagement but were prevented by a most violent Flood of Rain which continued all the day and following Night. When it held up, we had the mortification to find that our Ammunition, which had been completed to Forty Rounds, a Man, was intirely ruined..."[6]

Washington had no choice but to disengage. He marched his army towards a supply depot in Warwick. Maxwell's corps was ordered to remain behind and cover the removal of stores and baggage from Valley Forge.[7]

---

[5] Marshall, 307-308

[6] General Washington to John Hancock, 23 September, 1777 in *The Papers of George Washington Vol. 11*, 301

[7] General Washington to Brigadier General William Maxwell, 17 September, 1777 in *The Papers of George Washington Vol. 11*, 258

Another American force, under General Anthony Wayne, also stayed behind to harass the enemy's flanks and rear.[8] Wayne believed that Maxwell's corps had orders to act in conjunction with him. This was initially true, but unbeknownst to Wayne, those orders were changed, and Maxwell was ordered to help defend the fords over the Schuylkill River.[9]

General Wayne, however, operated under the mistaken belief that Maxwell's corps was within supporting distance of him. He paid dearly for this mistake on September 20th, when his division was surprised by a night bayonet attack. General Wayne lost nearly 300 men at the battle of Paoli. The enemy lost but a handful.[10]

General Howe resumed his advance the next day, maneuvering his army to threaten both an important supply depot at Reading, and the capital, Philadelphia. Washington responded by defending the approaches to Reading, but in doing so, he left the capital exposed. General Howe pounced on the opportunity. On September 23rd, the British crossed the Schuylkill River, the last natural barrier to Philadelphia. Three days later, they marched into the city unopposed.

General Washington had lost Philadelphia, but his army was still intact and he was eager to strike back. First, he reorganized the army. Maxwell's corps was disbanded, its men ordered back to their original units. It is unclear why this decision was made. Perhaps accusations of misconduct and lack of initiative, leveled against Maxwell by his subordinate officers, were a factor. Lieutenant Colonel Heth, clearly no supporter of Maxwell, wrote to his old commander, Colonel Morgan, about his dissatisfaction with Maxwell.

---

[8] General Washington to Brigadier General Wayne, 18 September, 1777 in *The Papers of George Washington Vol. 11*, 265
[9] Reed, 159-160
[10] Ibid. 176

"You have been greatly wished for since the Enemies Landing at the Head of Elk – Maxwell's Corps Twas expected would do great things – we had opportunities – and anybody but an old woman would have availd themselves of them – He is to be sure – A Damnd bitch of a General."[11]

The dissolution of the light corps allowed Captain Porterfield to return to his company in the 11th Virginia. His thoughts, however, were apparently on a different command. On October 3rd, General Washington forwarded a letter of recommendation to Governor Patrick Henry that was signed by some of the officers of Woodford's brigade. They called for Porterfield's promotion to a state artillery unit being raised in Virginia. The letter said,

"Captn Charles Porterfield; as an Officer of Virtue, & Abilities. The very early and disinterested part he took in the present dispute, is a proof of his Virtue. And his undaunted, and prudent Behaviour, as a Volunteer, at the Attack upon Quebec; compar'd with the more recent Instances, he has given as an Officer, have render'd his military Abilities equally indisputable. To this We wou'd beg leave to add, that his Inclination and Service have ever led him to the Study of the Mathematic, of which Gunnery constituties a part, & that We believe, a small Share of practice wou'd enable him to discharge with Credit, the duty requir'd of an Officer in that Line"[12]

---

[11] Heth Diary, 2 October, 1777, 33

[12] General Washington to Patrick Henry, 3 October, 1777 in *The Papers of George Washington Vol. 11*, 383

Included in Washington's letter to Governor Henry was a letter of recommendation for Captain Porterfield signed by Lt. Col. Richard Parker of the 2nd Virginia , Col. Thomas Marshall and Lt. Col. William Heth of the 3rd Virginia , Col. Alexander McClanachan of the 7th Virginia , and Lt. Col. Christian Febiger of the 11th Virginia.

General Washington did not personally know Captain Porterfield. His letter accompanying the recommendation, however, showed that he was acquainted with Porterfield's distinguished service. Washington wrote of Porterfield that,

> "...he is universally esteemed by his acquaintances in the Army as an Officer of very extraordinary merit."[13]

Although Washington forwarded the recommendation, he had little time to dwell on matters of rank. On the very day he wrote to Governor Henry, preparations were underway to attack the enemy.

Battle of Germantown

General Washington's plan was bold and complex. He hoped to repeat his success at Trenton by surprising the enemy's advance troops at Germantown, a village just north of Philadelphia. Like Trenton, Washington's plan called for a multi-pronged attack. He divided his 11,000 man army into four columns.[14]

They approached the British from the northwest along a twelve mile front. The two outer columns, consisting of 3,000 militia troops, were to swing around the British pickets and attack the enemy, *"in flank and rear"*.[15] The two center columns, comprising 8,000 continentals under Generals Sullivan and Greene, were to slam into the enemy's center. General Sullivan's column formed the right wing of the continentals and General Greene formed the left.

---

[13] Ibid. 382
[14] Marshall, 320
[15] General Orders for the Attack on Germantown, 3 October, 1777 in *The Papers of George Washington, Vol. 11*, 375

Each column received the same order, "...*to make their disposition so as to attack the* [enemy] *pickets in their respective routs, precisely at five O clock, with charged bayonets and without firing...*"[16]

Captain Porterfield and his regiment were assigned to General Greene's column. Their brigade (Woodford's) remained in General Steven's division, and held the extreme right flank of General Greene's column.[17] Greene's men had the longest route to march. They also had a poor guide who led them astry.[18] Consequently, Greene failed to launch his attack on time.

General Washington, who was with General Sullivan's column a few miles to the east, was unaware of Greene's difficulties and commenced the attack as planned. He described the initial fight in a letter to Congress.

"...*Genl Sullivans advanced party drawn from Conways Brigade attacked their picket at Mount Airy...about Sun rise...which presently gave way, and his Main body* [Sullivan's] *consisting of the right Wing, following soon engaged the* [enemy] *Light Infantry and Other Troops encamped near the picket which forced their Ground, leaving their Baggage. They retreated a considerable distance...*"[19]

While General Sullivan pressed the enemy, General Greene hurried his troops to the battle. They arrived forty-five minutes late. Washington noted, however, that once they joined the fight they were, *"for some time equally successful."*[20]

---

[16] Ibid, 376
[17] Marshall, 323
[18] Ward, 227
[19] General Washington to John Hancock, 5 October, 1777 in *The Papers of George Washington, Vol. 11,* 394
[20] Ibid.

As Greene's column engaged the enemy, heavy cannon and musket fire drew Woodford's brigade to the right.[21] The brigade was soon completely separated from General Stephen's division, and drawn instead, toward a battle for control of Benjamin Chew's stone mansion.

Although General Sullivan's men had already swept most of the British past the Chew mansion, over 100 soldiers of the 40th regiment barricaded themselves inside the building.[22] Its thick stone walls protected the British from much of the American fire. Nevertheless, the rebels were determined to take the house. A bloody struggle ensued, and Woodford's brigade headed straight for it.

When they arrived at the mansion, they joined in efforts to storm the building. The battle was intense and the noise drew the attention of Pennsylvania troops under General Anthony Wayne. They had already advanced several hundred yards past the house, but now feared that the British had somehow launched a counter-attack in their rear. They faced about and marched toward the Chew house to investigate.[23] The morning fog and smoke of battle reduced visibility to near zero. As Wayne's men marched back towards the Chew house, a battle line emerged through the smoke on their right. Suddenly a volley crashed into their flank. The Pennsylvanians wheeled to the right and responded with a volley of their own. Both lines assumed the other was the enemy. Both were wrong. In the chaos and confusion of battle General Stephen's Virginians had fired into General Wayne's Pennsylvanians. Wayne's men replied in kind. Stephen's men fired at least one more volley at the Pennsylvanians before the tragic mistake was discovered.

---

[21] Thomas McGuire, *The Surprise of Germantown: October 4th, 1777*, (Cliveden of the National Trust for Historic Preservation, 1994), 76
[22] Ibid. 49
[23] Ibid. 79

The number of casualties from this exchange is unknown. It is clear, however, that it impacted the American advance. The attack slowed and became disorganized. General Washington attributed much of the problem to the weather.

"The Morning was extremely foggy," he wrote, *"which prevented our improving the advantages we gained so well...This circumstance, by concealing from us the true situation of the Enemy, obliged us to act with more caution and less expedition than we could have wished, and gave the Enemy time to recover from the effects of our first impression..."*[24]

Despite these setbacks, Washington believed victory was still possible. However,

"in the midst of the most promising appearance – when every thing gave the most flattering hopes of victory, the Troops began suddenly to retreat; and entirely left the Field in spite of every effort that could be made to rally them."[25]

A number of factors converged to precipitate the American retreat. Many units ran out of ammunition. Others, due to the thick smoke and fog, lost contact with supporting units and feared they were about to be surrounded by the enemy. Still others faced the brunt of a strong British counterattack.[26] All of these factors led to an abrupt American withdrawal. The American retreat was so sudden and unexpected that the British suspected an American trap and pursued cautiously.[27]

---

[24] General Washington to John Hancock, 5 October, 1777, in *The Papers of George Washington, Vol. 11*, 394
[25] Ibid.
[26] McGuire, 83
[27] Ibid.

The battle of Germantown thus ended in another American defeat. American losses, estimated at over 1,000 men, were double the British.[28] However, the bold nature of the attack demonstrated that there was plenty of fight left in Washington's army. The capture of Philadelphia had not crushed the rebels' spirits. The American army remained intact and in the field, waiting for the next opportunity to strike.

Valley Forge

For the next two months Washington's army encamped at Whitemarsh, thirteen miles from Philadelphia. They were too weak to dislodge the entrenched British, yet, reluctant to end the campaign. General Howe, on the other hand, was content to let the Americans linger. He had accomplished his objective, namely, the capture of Philadelphia. The destruction of two American river forts, in mid November, created a secure supply line for the British via the Delaware River. If General Washington wished to remain in the field and expose his men to the hardships of winter, so be it. The British would spend a cozy winter in Philadelphia, and finish off the American's in the spring.

The Continental Congress was not pleased with these developments and urged General Washington to drive the British from the capital. Washington wished to oblige, but the more he examined the city's defenses, the more he realized the futility of such an attempt. His army was just too weak and exhausted to attack the fortified lines of the enemy. They could not remain in the field indefinitely, however. John Marshall noted that,

---

[28] McGuire, 87

"The cold was now becoming so intense that it was impossible for an army, neither well clothed, nor sufficiently supplied with blankets, to keep the field in tents."[29]

Thus, Washington decided to end the campaign and establish winter quarters at Valley Forge. He explained his decision in the general orders of December 17th. After praising the army for the, *"fortitude and patience with which they have sustained the fatigues of the Campaign,"* he explained his choice of Valley Forge for winter quarters.[30]

"The General ardently wishes, it were now in his power, to conduct the troops into the best winter quarters – But where are these to be found? Should we retire to the interior parts of the State, we should find them crowded with virtuous citizens, who, sacrificing their all, have left Philadelphia and fled thither for protection. To their distress humanity forbids us to add. This is not all, we should leave a vast extent of fertile country to be despoiled and ravaged by the enemy, from which they would draw vast supplies, and where many of our firm friends would be exposed to all the miseries of the most insulting and wanton depredation. A train of evils might be enumerated, but these will suffice. These considerations make it indispensibly necessary for the army to take such a position, as will enable it most effectually to prevent distress and to give the most extensive security; and in that position we must make ourselves the best shelter in our power. With activity and diligence Huts may be erected that will

---

[29] Marshall, 354

[30] General Orders for 17 December, 1777 in *The Papers of George Washington Vol. 12,* 620

be warm and dry. In these the troops will be compact, more secure against surprises than if in a divided state and at hand to protect the country. These cogent reasons have determined the General to take post in the neighbourhood of this camp; and influenced by them, he persuades himself, that the officers and soldiers, with one heart, and one mind, will resolve to surmount every difficulty, with a fortitude and patience, be coming their profession, and the sacred cause in which they are engaged. He himself will share in the hardship, and partake of every inconvenience."[31]

The next day's orders included instructions for the construction of the huts that would house the army. The men were placed in twelve man squads and a twelve dollar reward was offered to the first squad from each regiment that completed their hut.[32] The dimensions of the huts were specified.

"The Soldier's huts are to be of the following dimensions, viz: fourteen by sixteen each, sides, ends and roofs made with logs, and the roof made tight with split slabs, or in some other way; the sides made tight with clay, fire-place made of wood and secured with clay on the inside eighteen inches thick, this fireplace to be in the rear of the hut; the door to be in the end next the street; the doors to be made of split oak-slabs, unless boards can be procured. Side-walls to be six and a half feet high. The officers huts to form a line in the rear of the troops, one hut to be allowed to each General Officer, one to the Staff of

[31] Ibid. 620-621
[32] General Orders for 18 December, 1777 in *The Papers of George Washington Vol. 12*, 627

each brigade, one to the field officers of each regiment, one to the Staff of each regiment, one to the commissioned officers of two companies, and one to every twelve non-commissioned officers and soldiers."[33]

The men started building the huts as soon as they arrived at Valley Forge. They also began construction of the earthworks and redoubts that protected them for the next six months. An outer defense line was extended along a ridge from the Schuylkill River to the foot of Mount Joy. An inner defense line was also established.

Woodford's brigade was positioned on the extreme right of the outer line. The earthworks at this location wrapped around a hill, so that the far right of the outer line actually faced west rather than south. In other words, Woodford's brigade was positioned at a ninety degree angle to the rest of the outer line. It was an isolated position, tucked in a vale between Mt. Joy and the outer ridge. General Charles Scott's brigade of Virginians covered Woodford's left flank, but the rest of the outer line wrapped around the ridge and out of sight, extending towards the river for a mile.

When the army marched into Valley Forge, it was desperately low on provisions. Yet, they paused to observe a public day of thanksgiving, ordained by Congress. Joseph Plum Martin, a private from Connecticut, recalled the day in his memoirs.

"We had nothing to eat for two or three days previous, except that the trees of the fields and forests afforded us. But we must now have what Congress said, a sumptuous Thanksgiving to close the year of high living we had now nearly seen to a close...our country, ever mindful of its suffering army, opened

---

[33] Ibid. 627-628

her sympathizing heart so wide upon this occasion, as to give us something to make the world stare...it gave each and every man half a gill of rice and a tablespoon of vinegar!"[34]

Martin's complaints were echoed throughout the army. General James Varnum of Rhode Island reported to General Washington on December 22nd that,

"Three Days successively, we have been destitute of Bread. Two Days we have been intirely without Meat. – It is not to be had from Commissaries. – Whenever we procure Beef, it is of such a vile Quality, as to render it a poor Succedanium for Food. The Men must be supplied, or they cannot be commanded."[35]

General Washington passed the bad news on to Congress.

" I do not know from what cause this alarming deficiency, or rather total failure of Supplies arises: But unless more vigorous exertions and better regulations take place in that line and immediately, This Army must dissolve."[36]

The supply situation was so critical that Washington could not provision enough men to challenge an enemy foraging party. He bitterly complained to Congress.

---

[34] Joseph Plum Martin, *Private Yankee Doodle,* ed. George Scheer, (Eastern Acorn Press, 1998), 100
(Originally published in 1830)
[35] Joseph Lee Boyle, *Writings from the Valley Forge Encampment of the Continental Army Vol. 1,* (Bowie MD: Heritage Books Inc., 2000), 2
[36] General Washington to Henry Laurens, 22 December, 1777 in *The Papers of George Washington, Vol. 12,* 667

"[Upon] *receiving information that the Enemy, in force, had left the City...I ordered the Troops to be in readiness, that I might give every Opposition in my power; when behold! To my great mortification, I was not only informed, but convinced, that the Men were unable to stir on account of provision,* [lack of food] *and that a dangerous mutiny, begun the night before and which with difficulty was suppressed by the spirited exertions of some Officers, was still much to be apprehended for want of this Article."*[37]

The best General Washington could do was to send out a few small parties to watch and harass the enemy.[38]

Washington had called for the formation of such light parties a day earlier. Each brigade was ordered to,

"*furnish a good partisan Captain, two Subs.* [lieutenants] *three Serjeants, three Corporals, and fifty privates, all pickt men, fit for annoying the enemy in light parties."*[39]

Captain Porterfield commanded one of these light parties and may have even re-joined his old commander, Daniel Morgan, on the outskirts of the encampment.

Colonel Morgan and his depleted rifle corps (down to 170 men fit for service) had returned to the main army in mid November following their victorious exploits at Saratoga. They participated in several sharp skirmishes near the Whitemarsh encampment and, when the army moved to Valley Forge, were posted on one of the main approaches to the camp.

---

[37] General Washington to Henry Laurens, 23 December, 1777 in *The Papers of George Washington Vol. 12,* 683-684

[38] Ibid.

[39] General Orders, 22 December, 1777 in *The Papers of George Washington Vol. 12,* 664

On December 23rd Morgan, in two letters to General Washington, acknowledged the arrival of some of the newly formed light parties.

> *"We are reinforced by fifteen or sixteen detachments every one separate Commands...Several of the Captns of the Detach'd parties put themselves under my Command. I took Charge of them, fixed upon a place of randisvouz, and detach'd Companies to scout round the enemies lines...the other parties* [that did not join Morgan] *had no success, they are by no means fit for scouts...*[40]

Given Captain Porterfield's past association with Colonel Morgan, it is very likely that his detachment was one of six that joined Morgan's command.[41]

Unlike the independent detachments that Morgan complained about, Porterfield's men had some success against the enemy. On December 26th General Washington received news that,

> *"The Enemy had 5 or 6 Men killed in a Skirmish yesterday & several wounded by Capn Porterfield of Genl Woodfords Brigade whose little party I'm informed by those who were Spectators behaved exceedingly well – he had 2 or 3 Men killed."*[42]

---

[40] Daniel Morgan to General Washington, 23 December, 1777 in *The Papers of George Washington Vol. 12*, 690
[41] Major General Stirling to General Washington, 24 December, 1777 in *The Papers of George Washington Vol. 12*, 697
[42] Major John Clark Jr. to General Washington, 26 December, 1777 in *The Papers of George Washington Vol. 13*, 4

Porterfield, and his men, remained on the perimeter of the American camp until December 29th, when all of the detachments were ordered to return.[43]

They returned to a camp that was busy with activity. Huts were still being built, entrenchments dug, wood cut and fields of fire cleared. Captain Porterfield shared a hut with three lieutenants, John Marshall, Philip Slaughter, and his own brother, Robert Porterfield.[44]

Woodford's brigade, like the entire American army, was a mere shadow of its former self. Of the 1,287 men listed on the January brigade roll, only 231 were present and fit for duty.[45] Another two hundred men were on duty elsewhere, such as with Colonel Morgan's rifle corps. The rest of the men, a full two thirds of the brigade, were sick, on furlough, or unfit for duty because they lacked adequate clothing.[46] Such shortages in manpower placed a greater burden on those who remained in the ranks. Captain Porterfield, for instance, assumed command of Captain William Blackwell's company, as well as his own. Blackwell had to leave the army due to an illness.[47]

As February neared, Woodford's brigade shrank further. The two year enlistments of the 3rd and 7th Virginians expired, and those men headed home. Some men re-enlisted, but even they were allowed to go home on furlough. By the end of February, Woodford's brigade had a total of 119 men fit for duty, and only 57 of them were privates.[48]

---

[43] Major General Stirling to General Washington, 29 December, 1777 in *The Papers of George Washington Vol. 13*, 52

[44] Reverend Philip Slaughter, *A History of St. Mark's Parish*, (1877), 108

[45] Charles H. Lesser, ed. *The Sinews of Independence: Monthly Strength Reports of the Continental Army*, (Chicago: The University of Chicago Press, 1976), 58

[46] Ibid.

[47] Charles Cullen and Herbert Johnson, eds. *The Papers of John Marshall Vol. 1*, (University of North Carolina Press, 1977), 12

[48] Lesser, 59

These men endured the worst part of Valley Forge. The supply system, which barely functioned in January, completely failed in February.

> "*A moments Opportunity presents of telling you our Distress in Camp has been infinite,*" wrote Alexander Scammell on February 19th. "*In all the Scenes since I have been in the army, want of provisions these ten Days past, has been the most distressing; [a] great part of our Troops 7 Days with only half a pound of Pork during the whole time –Our poor brave Soldiers living upon bread & water & naked exhibited a Sight exceedingly affecting to the Officers.*"[49]

William Weeks, the paymaster of the 3rd New Hampshire Regiment, expressed similar concerns.

> "*The first thing I must enter upon is the Scarcity of Provision here. Death seem'd to stare the poor Soldiers in the Face; for this five Days the Soldiers have not drawn [a] Tenth Part of their Allowance.*"[50]

Even General Washington noted the hardship, writing to George Clinton, of New York, for assistance.

> "*It is with great reluctance, I trouble you on a subject, which does not properly fall within your province; but it is a subject that occasions me more distress, than I have felt, since the commencement of the war...I mean the present dreadful situation of the army for want of provisions, and the miserable*

---

[49] Joseph Lee Boyle, *Writings from the Valley Forge Encampment of the Continental Army Vol. 2*, (Bowie MD: Heritage Books Inc., 2001), 50
[50] Boyle, *Writings from the Valley Forge Encampment of the Continental Army Vol. 1*, 55

prospects before us, with respect to futurity...For some days past, there has been little less, than a famine in camp. A part of the army has been a week, without any kind of flesh, and the rest three or four days. Naked and starving as they are, we cannot enough admire the incomparable patience and fidelity of the soldiery, that they have not been ere this excited by their sufferings, to a general mutiny and dispersion. Strong symptoms, however, of discontent have appeared in particular instances; and nothing but the most active efforts every where can long avert so shocking a catastrophe."[51]

Thankfully, the crisis passed when more provisions found their way to camp.

The approach of spring brought a surge of men to the ranks. General Woodford's brigade swelled to 470 men fit for duty, and the 11th Virginia accounted for 123 of them.[52] By June, the brigade numbered almost 650 men, with nearly a quarter of them coming from the 11th regiment. Warmer weather also led to a change in the camp routine. Work on the entrenchments continued, as did fatigue and guard duty. But the arrival of Baron von Steuben, from Europe, meant that the men soon learned a new military drill.

Steuben arrived in Valley Forge in late February and immediately impressed General Washington with his military knowledge and humility.[53] Washington asked the Baron to assess the American army.[54] Steuben's observations were the beginning of significant reforms for the American army.

---

[51] General Washington to George Clinton, 16 February, 1778, in *The Papers of George Washington Vol. 13*, 552-553
[52] Lesser, 72
[53] John W. Jackson, *Valley Forge: Pinnacle of Courage*, (Gettysburg, PA: Thomas Publications, 1992), 124
[54] Ibid. 126

"I directed my attention to the condition of the troops," recalled Steuben years later, *"and found ample field, where disorder and confusion were supreme...the words company, regiment, brigade, and division, were so vague that they did not convey any idea upon which to form a calculation...I have seen a regiment consisting of thirty men, and a company of one corporal!"*[55]

Steuben was particularly critical of the haphazard system of drill the army employed.

"Each colonel had a system of his own, the one according to the English, the other according to the Prussian or French style."[56]

His keen observations prompted General Washington to ask him to oversee the implementation of reforms. Steuben immediately went to work. John Marshall summarized Baron von Steuben's impact on the American army.

"This gentleman was a real service to the American troops. He established one uniform system of field exercise; and, by his skill and persevering industry, effected important improvements through all ranks of the army during its continuance at Valley Forge."[57]

The army got a chance to demonstrate these improvements in late June, upon the battlefield of Monmouth, New Jersey.

---

[55] Friedrich Kapp, *The Life of Frederick William von Steuben*, (NY: Corner House Historical Publications, 1999), 115
(Originally published in 1859)
[56] Ibid. 118
[57] Marshall, 439

Chapter Six

Monmouth to Virginia

Rumors circulated through Valley Forge as early as spring that the British planned to evacuate Philadelphia. The city's capture, back in September, did not bring the Americans to the bargaining table. In fact, Congress spurned British peace overtures that effectively gave America everything it demanded before 1776. Parliament renounced its right to tax, or even rule over the colonies, except on issues of trade.[1] For the Americans, however, nothing short of independence would do.

The lack of progress in the dispute cost General Howe his command. He returned to Britain, in May, to defend his actions. General Henry Clinton replaced Howe and was immediately confronted with a new strategic problem, France's entry into the war.

News of the American alliance with France bolstered American spirits and caused the British to re-think their strategy. Britain could no longer depend on complete dominance of the sea. Furthermore, her other global possessions were potential targets and had to be protected. This stretched British resources and drew needed men and supplies away from America.

The British, concerned that their forces were overextended, decided to consolidate around New York. Preparations for Philadelphia's evacuation began in May. By June 18th, Clinton's army, along with thousands of loyalist civilians, was on the move. A portion of the army, and many of the

---

[1] William Stryker, *The Battle of Monmouth*, William Starr Myers ed., (Princeton: Princeton Univ. Press, 1927), 35

loyalists, departed the city by ship. The remainder, numbering over 10,000 men, marched through New Jersey.[2]

General Washington, with nearly 11,000 men, began a cautious pursuit of the British.[3] He sent Colonel Morgan's rifle corps, bolstered to 600 men, to harass the right flank of the enemy.[4] Three other large detachments, under generals William Maxwell, Charles Scott, and Anthony Wayne, were also sent forward to pressure the enemy.

Washington offered overall command of the advanced detachments to General Charles Lee. General Lee, who returned to the American army in April (after sixteen months of captivity in New York) initially declined the command. Concern for his reputation, however, caused him to reverse himself, and he took charge of approximately 5,000 men (almost half the American army).[5]

The main body of the army, including most of General Woodford's brigade, trailed about five miles behind Lee's advanced corps. A field return for June 28th reported 385 privates fit for duty in Woodford's brigade. Nine captains were also listed.[6] It is difficult to say if Captain Porterfield was one of those captains. Six days earlier, General Washington ordered each brigade to send, *"an active, spirited officer and 25 of its best marksmen,"* to join Colonel Morgan's rifle corps and harass the enemy flank.[7] It is possible that Porterfield was selected to join Morgan's corps. If so, it

---

[2] Mark M. Boatner III, *Encyclopedia of the American Revolution, 3rd. Ed.* (Stackpole Books, 1994), 716   (Originally published in 1966)
[3] Council of War, 24 June, 1778 in *The Writings of George Washington, Vol. 12,* 116
[4] General Orders, 22 June, 1778 in *The Writings of George Washington Vol. 12,* 106
[5] Stryker, 80, 100-101
[6] "Field Return of Troops under the immediate command of his Excellency Gen'l Washington, 28 June, 1778 in Stryker's *The Battle of Monmouth,* 120
[7] General Orders, June 22, 1778 in *The Writings of George Washington Vol. 12,* 106

means he missed most of the fighting at Monmouth, because on the day of the battle, Morgan received contradictory orders that kept him away from the action.

Whether Captain Porterfield actually fought at Monmouth is unclear. What is clear, however, is that the men of his regiment and brigade did fight there, and they played a vital role.

The Battle of Monmouth

The battle of Monmouth occurred in phases. It began on the morning of June 28th when General Lee's advanced corps engaged the rear guard of the British. Although Lee initially expressed reservations to Washington about attacking the British, his first reports seemed confident of success. He even sent word to Washington that he hoped to cut off the enemy's entire rear guard.[8]

Unfortunately, Lee's plan quickly unraveled because he failed to adequately inform his field commanders of his intentions. Lee's orders were vague and sporadic. As a result, his subordinates issued orders with little understanding of Lee's overall plan. Such poor communication led to confusion and misjudgments on the field. For instance, when General Lee repositioned his troops on the right flank, it was interpreted by his subordinates on the left as a retreat. These subordinates, namely Generals Charles Scott and Anthony Wayne, reacted to the apparent retreat of the American right wing by withdrawing their own men. Soon, the whole affair became confused. To make matters worse, General Clinton sent a large reinforcement to assist his rear guard. The arrival of these enemy reinforcements increased the anxiety of the Americans, who now feared they were fighting the whole British army. The situation became so confused that General Lee had to withdraw his entire corps.

---

[8] Stryker, 134

General Washington, who started the day with the main body of the army, heard the fighting and rode ahead to investigate. Based on General Lee's initial reports, he expected to find his advance troops pressing the enemy. Instead, he found them retreating in disorder. Washington angrily confronted General Lee, who tried to explain his actions. He then took personal command of the situation.

Washington needed to delay the enemy's advance long enough to allow his main force to form in the rear. He ordered Colonel Walter Stewart's 13th Pennsylvania, Lieutenant Colonel Nathaniel Ramsey's 3rd Maryland, and a composite Virginia regiment (the combined 4th, 8th, and 12th regiments) to make a stand in a patch of woods along the road.[9] General Anthony Wayne described what happened.

> *"...His Excellency...Ordered me to keep post where he met us with Stewart & [Ramsey's] Regiments and a Virginia Regt....then under my Command with two pieces of Artillery and to keep [the Enemy] in play until he had an [opportunity] of forming the Remainder of the Army and Restoring order – we had but just taken post when the Enemy began their attack with Horse, foot, & Artillery, the fire of their whole united force Obliged us after a Severe Conflict to give way..."[10]*

The American stand at the Point of Woods was determined, but brief. They were overwhelmed in a matter of minutes. Many of the men retreated to the main body of troops. Others, however, joined a second American line along a hedge row

---

[9] John Rees, *"What is this you have been about to day?"* : The New Jersey Brigade at the Battle of Monmouth (2003)
(Accessed via http://www.revwar75.com in the Complete Works of John U. Rees / New Jersey Brigade)
[10] Anthony Wayne to his wife, 1 July, 1778, in *Lee Papers, Vol. 2*, (New York Historical Society, 1871), 448-449

fence. This line was also formed to delay the British advance. Colonel John Laurens, an aide to General Washington, described the battle at the hedge line.

"Two regiments were formed behind a [hedge] fence...The enemy's horse advanced in full charge with admirable bravery to the distance of forty paces, when a general discharge from these regiments did great execution among them, and made them fly with the greatest precipitation."[11]

The unsuccessful British cavalry attack was followed by a frontal assault by British grenadiers. They too were repulsed and their commander, Colonel Henry Monckton, died in the charge. Colonel Laurens, reported that, *"In this spot the action was the hottest and there was considerable slaughter of the British Grenadiers."*[12] Despite the set back, however, the grenadiers reformed their lines and attacked again. The pressure on the Americans became too great, and they retreated across a ravine to the main American line.

Over the next few hours one of the most intense artillery duels of the war occurred. Both sides pounded the other (with limited effect). The Americans eventually gained an advantage when they placed four cannon on a hill (Combs Hill) that overlooked the left flank of the British line. This battery was supported by General Woodford's brigade, and it delivered a very effective enfilade fire upon the enemy. The British position became untenable and they withdrew from the ridge.

Their withdrawal, however, did not end the fight. General Wayne led three Pennsylvania regiments towards the position vacated by the enemy. This caused the British to halt their

---

[11] John Laurens to Henry Laurens, 30 June, 1778 in *Lee Papers, Vol. 2*, (New York Historical Society, 1871), 431-434

[12] Ibid.

retreat and return to the fight. General Wayne described the engagement.

> "...the Enemy began to Advance again in a heavy [column], against which I ordered some [blank] & advanced with some of my [troops] to meet them –the Action was Exceedingly warm and well Maintained on each side for a Considerable time."[13]

Eventually, both sides disengaged and withdrew, leaving the ground littered with bodies.

Fighting occurred on the American left as well, most notably around the Sutfin house. In the late afternoon, British troops advanced toward the American line and took position in an orchard. A party of Americans, numbering over 600 and commanded by Colonels Joseph Cilley and Richard Parker, worked their way through a morass to strike the British on their flank. General Stirling described the action.

> "I then detached Col: Sealy [Cilley] with 400 men supported by Col. Parker with 250 along the Ravene on my left in order to gain the Enemy's Right, this they effected with so much address that they were within 100 yards of the Enemy before they were discovered; they immediately directed their fire so well & so briskly that the British Grenadiers & Royal Highlanders were obliged to show their backs."[14]

As evening approached, General Washington attempted one last strike at the enemy. He ordered the brigades of

---

[13] Anthony Wayne to his wife, 1 July, 1778, in *Lee Papers, Vol. 2*, 448-449

[14] Major General William Alexander, Lord Stirling, to William H. Drayton, 15 August, 1778 in "Letters of William Alexander, Lord Stirling," *Proceedings of the New Jersey Historical Society, Vol. 60, no. 3* (July 1942), 173-174

General Woodford and General Poor to attack the enemy's flanks. Neither brigade was able to do so, however, before darkness descended.

The battle of Monmouth thus ended in stalemate. Both armies remained on the field and both claimed victory. The British believed they fought a successful rear guard action that repulsed the Americans and protected their baggage train. The Americans countered with the claim that they inflicted heavy losses on the British. Furthermore, the late night withdrawal of the British left the Americans in sole possession of the field. This all too rare occurrence infused the American army with pride. General Washington expressed his pleasure with the army's conduct in the following day's general orders.

> *"The Commander in Chief congratulates the Army on the Victory obtained over the Arms of his Britanick Majesty yesterday and thanks most sincerely the gallant officers and men who distinguished themselves upon the occasion and such others as by their good order and coolness gave the happiest presages of what might have been expected had they come to Action."* [15]

The battle of Monmouth marked a new milestone for General Washington's army. In the longest engagement of the war, they fought the British to a standstill. They endured near 100 degree heat, and held the battlefield (while the enemy scampered off to New York in the middle of the night).

Casualties are difficult to determine with certainty, but estimates for both sides are strikingly similar, approximately 350 men each. Total losses for the British in the march across New Jersey exceeded 1,000 men, due in large part to over 600 deserters. [16]

---

[15] General Orders, 29 June, 1778, in *The Writings of Washington, Vol. 12*, 130

[16] Boatner III, 725

Monmouth was the last major battle in the north. The British concentrated their forces around New York and re-evaluated their strategy. Within a year, their attention shifted to the south. In the meantime, the American and British armies around New York remained largely stationary. The men on both sides probably appreciated the respite. At the same time, however, inactivity meant that the dispute went unresolved, and their duty as soldiers dragged on.

New Duties

Two weeks after the battle, Captain Porterfield was named brigade major of General Woodford's brigade.[17] Brigade majors assisted in the management of the brigade. They received daily orders from the adjutant-general and relayed the orders to the regimental adjutants. Brigade majors also helped oversee that the orders were properly executed.

While Captain Porterfield adjusted to his new responsibilities, word arrived from Virginia that he was appointed Major of a new state garrison regiment.[18] Virginia established this new unit, *"for garrisoning the fortifications and batteries erected for the defense of the several ports and harbours* [of the state]."[19] This meant that the duty station of the regiment was limited to the state's borders. In fact, a provision in the law that created the regiment specified that,

> *"If any person enlisted for the said battalion shall at any time be ordered to march out of the commonwealth, such order shall amount to a discharge."*[20]

---

[17] General Orders, 13 July, 1778, *The Writings of Washington, Vol. 12,* 176

[18] H.R. McIlwaine, ed., *Journals of the Council of the State of Virginia, Vol. 2,* (Richmond: Virginia State Library, 1932), 153

[19] William H. Hening, *The Statutes at Large Being a Collection of all the Laws of Virginia, Vol. 9,* (Richmond: George Cochran, 1821), 452

[20] Ibid.

Since the unit had yet to recruit its first soldier, the regiment's officers were told not to leave their current military posts until they were summoned by the state. Major Porterfield, who was still a captain in the Continental army, thus remained with Woodford's brigade for the rest of 1778.

In August, he was reunited with his original commander, Colonel Daniel Morgan. After Monmouth, the twenty five "select" men from each brigade that joined Morgan's rifle corps returned to their brigades. Only a hundred or so men remained in Morgan's rifle corps. That was too few for an officer of his rank to command, so the rifle corps was re-organized into a two company rifle detachment and placed under the command of Major Thomas Posey of the 7th Virginia Regiment.[21]

Colonel Morgan returned to the 11th Virginia. He also temporarily commanded the 15th Virginia Regiment. This was brief, however, because in September, General Washington re-organized the Virginia Line (the sixteen continental regiments from Virginia were reduced to twelve). Regiments were merged and re-numbered and many officers found themselves with new commands. The 11th Virginia, for instance, was renamed the 7th Virginia and the 15th regiment became the 11th. Colonel Morgan thus became commander of the "new" 7th Virginia Regiment. The old 7th Virginia was renamed the 5th Virginia.[22]

Captain Porterfield, and his company, remained under Morgan's command in the "new" 7th regiment. They also remained in General Woodford's brigade. For the rest of 1778

---

[21] Tench Tilghman to Thomas Posey, 18 July, 1778 in *George Washington Papers* at the Library of Congress, 1741-1799: Series 4, (Online at www.loc.gov

[22] E.M. Sanchez-Saavedra, *A Guide to Virginia Military Organizations in the American Revolution, 1774-1787*, (Willow Bend Books: Westminster, MD, 1978), 52

Porterfield balanced his company commander responsibilities with his duties as brigade major.

In October, Colonel Morgan assumed command of the entire brigade, temporarily replacing General Woodford, who returned to Virginia on furlough.[23] It appears that sometime in December or early January, Captain Porterfield also returned to Virginia. On January 8th, 1779 his duties as brigade major were transferred to his brother, Robert.

"Lieutenant Robert Porterfield of the 7th Virginia Regiment is to do the duty of Brigade Major 'till further orders in General Woodford's Brigade, Brigade Major Porterfield being absent."[24]

Charles Porterfield's absence marked the close of his involvement with the Continental Army. Although he did not resign his continental commission until July 1779, Porterfield's participation in the continental army ceased when he returned to Virginia.[25]

Porterfield's activities between January and March, 1779, are difficult to determine. It is likely that his absence began as a long overdue furlough in Virginia. Sometime in the spring

---

[23] See: General Washington to Peter Muhlenberg, 28 October, 1778 and General Washington to Daniel Morgan, 25 November, 1778 in The Writings of George Washington from the Original Manuscripts, 1745-1799, John C. Fitzpatrick, ed., (Online at www.loc.gov)
Note: On October 28, 1778 General Washington wrote to General Peter Muhlenberg, stating that, *"Genl. Woodford is already gone to Virginia."* On November 25, 1778 General Washington wrote to Colonel Morgan, instructing him to, *"receive directions from the Quarter Master General for the position of the Brigade under your command."*

[24] General Orders, 8 January, 1779, in *The Writings of Washington, Vol. 13,* 485
[25] See Note 74 in William Alexander, Lord Stirling, General Orders, 8 January, 1779 in *The Writings of George Washington From the Original Manuscript Sources,* (Online at www.loc.gov)

of 1779, he was promoted to lieutenant colonel of the state garrison regiment.[26]

It is unclear, however, when he assumed his command responsibilities. One account of Porterfield's whereabouts placed him in Williamsburg in late May. Apparently Lieutenant Colonel Porterfield, and several comrades, paid a visit to Governor Thomas Jefferson at the Governor's Palace. Baylor Hill, of the First Continental Light Dragoons, recorded the visit in his diary.

May 30th 1779

This morning I breakfast wth Col. Porterfield at the Barracks and after; we went to town and at nine o' clock I went in company of several to a Tavern near the College to drink punch where we were join[ed] by others on the same business and by Eleven o' Clock the whole Company was very happy. And at breaking up the society, we concluded to pay the Governor a visit; upon wch Capt D...was to go for'd and inform him of our intentions. Col. Porterfield being the oldest officer present, he took the Command, and march[ed us] in the best for his detachment amounting in the whole to eleven, into the Pallace, where we were reciev'd by his Excelency in Person, we staid and see the last of a very large bowl of Grogg, and then we beet a march to the barracks In and about William's burg...[27]

---

[26] McIlwaine, 254-255
References to Major Edward Waller of the State Garrison Regiment and Col. Porterfield suggest that Porterfield was promoted to Lt. Col. sometime prior to April 5, 1779 and that Waller was promoted from captain to major of the same regiment.
[27] John T. Hayes, ed., *A Gentleman of Fortune, The Diary of Baylor Hill, First Continental Light Dragoons, 1777-1781, Vol. 2,* (Saddlebagg Press, 1995), 56-58

A few days later, Porterfield participated in a more serious activity, namely, a Court of Inquiry.[28] This activity, coupled with his resignation from the continental army in July, suggest that he assumed his command duties in the state garrison regiment sometime during the summer.

By October, 1779, Porterfield's new unit numbered less than 200 men, with 138 privates, 22 non-commissioned officers, and only three captains.[29] It stationed small detachments in Williamsburg, Yorktown, Hampton, and Portsmouth. For most of 1779, duty in the garrison regiment was uneventful. In December, however, reports that a large British fleet was heading to Virginia created anxiety in the government. Six months earlier, the state suffered significant material losses at the hands of a brief British raid. Governor Jefferson was determined to prevent another such disaster and called the militia out in force.

Colonel Porterfield's regiment was ordered to escort British prisoners from Williamsburg to King William County.[30] This proved unnecessary however, because the British bypassed Virginia and headed to South Carolina instead. Although Virginia was temporarily spared more destruction, events in South Carolina had enormous consequences for the state, and Charles Porterfield.

---

[28] *Virginia Gazette*, 19 June, 1779, Dixon and Nicholson
[29] Returns of Virginia Land and Naval Forces, 1 October, 1779, *in The Papers of Thomas Jefferson, Vol. 3*, 254 (page 3 insert)
[30] John Selby, *The Revolution in Virginia, 1775-1783*, (Colonial Williamsburg Foundation: Williamsburg, VA, 1988), 211

Chapter Seven

Road to Camden

General Clinton and the British, embracing a new southern strategy, set their sights on Charleston, South Carolina. In response, the Virginia legislature adopted a new law that empowered the Governor to send up to 1,500 militia and, *"so many of the state troops as can be marched thither, according to the terms of their enlistments, or are willing to march...to the assistance of the said state of South Carolina."*[1] Little amounted of this assistance, however, until February, 1780.

On February 18th, the Virginia Board of War proposed that a relief detachment for South Carolina be formed from among the state troops.[2] That same day, Governor Jefferson wrote to Colonel George Muter, the commander of the state garrison regiment, informing Muter of his plans to send,

> *"the whole of our regiment of artillery (whom we have a power of sending out of the state) and a detachment from yours of about 80 under the command of Colo. Porterfield, with the two state troops of horse."*[3]

Jefferson concluded the letter by asking Colonel Muter to,

> *"communicate to Colo. Porterfield an order to prepare immediately for marching, and to concert*

---

[1] Hening, Vol. 10, 214

[2] From the Board of War, 18 February, 1780, in *The Papers of Thomas Jefferson, Vol. 3,* 299

[3] Governor Jefferson to George Muter, 18 February, 1780, in *The Papers of Thomas Jefferson, Vol. 3,* 301-302

with him the best means of obtaining voluntarily the number of men required from your battalion."[4]

Jefferson acknowledged that many of the garrison troops had re-enlisted under provisions that now allowed them to be sent out of the state. But, wrote Jefferson, *"we would rather call the willing into service."*[5]

Within two weeks, sixty volunteers from the state garrison regiment joined the relief detachment.[6] A month later Colonel Porterfield received word from the Board of War that he was,

> *"...to command the detachment of Virginia troops, consisting of volunteers of the State Garrison Regiment, the greater part of* [Colonel Thomas] *Marshall's Corps of Artillery and two Troops of* [Major John] *Nelsons horse, to be under Porterfield's absolute controul and Command and to be prepared to march on the Shortest notice to Charleston, S.C."*[7]

There was a degree of urgency in these preparations because the news from South Carolina was grim. A large British force landed near Charleston in February and gradually advanced on the town. By April, Charleston was besieged. Among the town's defenders were the bulk of Virginia's continental troops, sent to Charleston in December, 1779 and commanded by General William Woodford. [8]

Despite many signs that their position was untenable, the American commander at Charleston, General Benjamin

---

[4] Ibid. 302

[5] Ibid.

[6] From the Board of War, 3 March, 1780, in *The Papers of Thomas Jefferson, Vol. 3,* 307

[7] Board of War to Charles Porterfield, 29 March, 1780 in *The Papers of Thomas Jefferson, Vol. 3,* 337

[8] John Buchanan, *The Road to Guilford Courthouse: The American Revolution in the Carolina,* (John Wiley & Sons, Inc. : NY, 1997), 56-57

Lincoln, heeded the pleas and threats of civilian authorities and remained in the town. By late April the last escape route out of Charleston was blocked.

The distressing situation in South Carolina did not hamper the recruitment of volunteers for Porterfield's corps, however. When they began their march to Charleston (from Williamsburg in late April) the detachment numbered over 450 men.[9] It included two troops of cavalry (numbering sixty four men) and almost 400 infantry (from the state garrison and artillery regiments). Although the state artillery regiment contributed the largest number of men (over 275), it appears that the men served as infantry troops.[10] A little over half the detachment, specifically those whose enlistment extended beyond September 30th, was placed on continental establishment.[11]

When Porterfield's corps arrived in Hillsborough, North Carolina, in late May, they received the stunning news that General Lincoln had surrendered Charleston.[12] This marked the biggest American defeat of the war. The American militia in Charleston were granted their parole and allowed to return home. The continentals, however, including Colonel Porterfield's brother, Robert, remained in the city as prisoners of war.

Despite the bad news, Porterfield's corps pressed forward. A few days later they received another shock. Colonel Abraham Buford's detachment of 350 Virginian continentals, on their way back from a failed attempt to re-enforce the

---

[9] State of the Virginia Forces, 2 May, 1780 in *The Papers of Thomas Jefferson, Vol. 3,* 364-365
[10] Estimate of Troops for South Carolina, 29 March, 1780, in *The Papers of Thomas Jefferson, Vol. 3,* 338
[11] State of the Virginia Forces, 2 May, 1780 in *The Papers of Thomas Jefferson, Vol. 3,* 364-365
[12] John Denton Pension Application, in *Virginia Revolutionary Pension Applications, Vol. 29,* Abstracted and Compiled by John Frederick Dorman, (Washington, D.C., 1977), 37

Charleston garrison, was annihilated by the British Legion. The clash occurred near the border of North and South Carolina. Although Colonel Banastre Tarleton's Legion was outnumbered, they cut the Virginians to pieces.[13] Many of Buford's men tried to surrender, but few prisoners were taken. Over 100 Virginians were killed and 150 wounded, most severely. Colonel Buford and about fifty men were all that escaped the slaughter.[14]

When Colonel Porterfield received news of Buford's defeat, he reversed direction and headed north. On June 2nd, North Carolina Governor John Rutledge wrote to Governor Jefferson with news of Porterfield's whereabouts.

> *"Colo. Porterfield thinking his force insufficient to oppose the enemy, retreated yesterday from this town* [Salisbury NC] *and crossed the Yadkin* [River], *meaning however to return and join the militia here, if they turn out in such numbers as may probably be able to prevent the enemy's getting higher up the Country.*[15]

Porterfield's corps continued on to Guilford Courthouse and then Hillsborough, where, *"after camping there a few days they took up the line of march for Virginia..."*[16] They were only on the march for a few hours, however, when they met General Baron De Kalb, marching south with a contingent of Maryland and Delaware continentals. Porterfield joined De Kalb and returned to Hillsborough.

It had been a difficult journey for De Kalb's continentals. The heat, insects, and toil of a summer march in the south

---

[13] Buchanan, 82
[14] Ibid. 83
[15] John Rutledge to Jefferson, 2 June, 1780, in *The Papers of Thomas Jefferson, Vol. 3*, 415
[16] Denton Pension Application, 37

exhausted the men. As a result, De Kalb remained in Hillsborough for over a week to allow his men to recuperate. On June 30th, De Kalb resumed his movement south. Provisions were a major concern for the army, however, and after only five days, they halted for lack of food. They were stuck on the southern bank of the Deep River for two weeks. One soldier described the ordeal.

"We marched from Hillsborough about the 1st of July, without an once of provision being laid in at any point, often fasting for several days together, and subsisting frequently upon green apples and peaches; sometimes by detaching parties, we thought ourselves feasted when by violence they seized a little fresh beef and cut and threshed out a little wheat;"[17]

On July 19th, the newly appointed commander of the southern army, General Horatio Gates, wrote to Governor Jefferson about the distressing situation.

"An officer just from the Baron's Head Quarters has assured me that there are Intervals of 24 Hours – in which the Army without Distinction are obliged to feed upon such Green Vegetables as they can find, having neither Animal Food or Corn.—So frequent and total a Want must eventually break up our Camp."[18]

It is unclear if Colonel Porterfield and his men suffered with General De Kalb's men at Deep River. Porterfield's corps was significantly reduced in July and the men who

---

[17] Christopher L. Ward, *The Delaware Continentals, 1776-1783*, (Wilmington: The Historical Society of Delaware, 1941), 333
[18] From Horatio Gates, 19 July, 1780, in *The Papers of Thomas Jefferson, Vol. 3*, 496

remained spent at least part of the month on detached service. Porterfield's corps shrank for several reasons. The enlistments of nearly 175 of his men expired over the summer.[19] Seventy artillerists from this group were discharged in mid July alone.[20] The remaining artillerymen were incorporated into General De Kalb's artillery. Additionally, Porterfield's cavalry was in such bad condition that they were sent to Halifax to refit and recruit.[21] By August, only 100 infantrymen remained under Porterfield's command.

It appears that this small corps was away from camp when General Gates arrived on July 25th. Two days later, Gates commenced a march to Camden, South Carolina. Against the advice of his subordinate commanders, he chose the most direct route to Camden, marching the army through a barren land, devoid of adequate provision. The men once again lived on green corn and unripe peaches. Soup was thickened with the hair powder of officers.[22] A soldier from Delaware noted in his journal that,

> *"At this time we were so much distressed for want of provisions, that we were fourteen days and drew but one half pound of flour. Sometimes we drew half a pound of beef per man and that so miserably poor that scarce any mortal could make use of it – living chiefly on green apples and peaches, which rendered our situation truly miserable, being in a weak and*

---

[19] Estimate of Troops for South Carolina, 29 March, 1780, in *The Papers of Thomas Jefferson, Vol. 3*, 338

[20] John Dean Pension Application, in *Virginia Revolutionary Pension Applications, Vol. 28*, Abstracted and Compiled by John Frederick Dorman, (Washington, D.C., 1977), 69

[21] Baron De Kalb, to Major Genl. Gates, 16 July, 1780, in *The State Records of North Carolina 1779-1780, Vol. 14*, Walter Clark ed., (Winston: M.I. & J.C. Stewart, Printers to the State, 1896), 504

[22] Christopher Ward, 337

sickly condition, and surrounded on all sides by our enemies the Tories."[23]

Colonel Porterfield's corps, still detached from the army, helped alleviate some of the distress by collecting cattle. On August 4th, he informed General Gates about his find.

"Agreeable To Your orders I marched To this place [Thompson's Creek] *& dispatched a Trusty Sergt. to Major Jackson of the Militia for his assistance, & expect by the Time You come up he will have a considerable number of Cattle at this place. I have shut up five fit for beef in a pasture Just over the Creeks on the right hand.*"[24]

General Gates, impressed by Porterfield's abilities, augmented his small corps with a contingent of light troops from General Caswell's North Carolina militia. This disappointed Lieutenant Colonel Charles Armand, who had requested that both Caswell's light troops and Porterfield's infantry be assigned to his cavalry command. Armand expressed his disappointment to General Gates on August 8th.

"The day before yesterday I made application to your Excellency to have some foots of the militia attached to my command until the infantry of Major Lee could joyn the army...your Excellency Had been pleased to consider the matter, and in consequence Had reinforced my command with one Hundred and fifty of the militia and Lnt. Col. Porterfield's men. I expected that this should be my constant command till the foot men of Lee should arrive. However, Col.

---

[23] Ibid. 338
[24] Col. Porterfield to Major Gen. Gates, 4 August, 1780, in *The State Records of North Carolina 1779-1780, Vol. 14,* 533

Porterfield Has, as it is seen, received particular orders to march, and has march[ed] this evening, without I knew nothing of it; and it seems, by a Conversation that I Had with Col. Porterfield, that he looked upon those militia men as under His immediate command. However, it was me who made an application to your Excellency and Genl. Caswel for those men."[25]

Armand emphasized that his complaint was not a criticism of Porterfield's abilities but rather, a result of his desire to supplement his own unit with desperately needed infantry.

"I beg your Excellency would not believe that I mean to complain in the least of Col. Porterfield, whose character I respect and whose Happiness and command I am far to be Jaleous of..."[26]

It was fortunate that Lieutenant Colonel Armand held no jealousy towards Porterfield because on the same day he wrote to Gates, the General placed Armand and his cavalry under Porterfield's command. Porterfield was instructed to take his re-enforced corps and press forward.

"You will be pleased to proceed immediately on the Rout which the Enemy have taken, with the Virginia Troops, the Light Infantry of General Caswell's Division, and the Detachment of Cavalry which is ordered to join you, under your Command. Your object will be to hang upon the Enemy's Rear; to harass them as much as lies in your Power, and to take every Advantage which Circumstances may

---

[25] Lt. Col. Armand to Maj. Gen. Gates, 8 August, 1780 in *The State Records of North Carolina 1779-1780, Vol. 14,* 536-537
[26] Ibid.

offer. I place so entire a Confidence in your Military Abilities, Prudence and Courage, that I leave the conduct of your operations altogether to your own Discretion, not doubting that you will distress the Enemy as much as lies in your Power; without hazarding too much the Troops under your Command."[27]

Porterfield found himself in a familiar position, the advance guard of the army. On August 9th he reported his progress to General Gates.

"I have the Honour To inform You I arrived at Lynche's Creeks by 10 O'Clocke at night, & found the Bridge Takun up & plankes thrown in the creeke. By the assistance of the Fence rails we soon replaced them & I was informed...that the British left this place about 5 O'Clocke, in the time of the rain, & that they intended halting at Widow Kelly's, two miles distant. This I found True. I advanced with the Horse and part of the Infantry To a ravine on the Road Laying in front of their camp, which I could see by the fires & to be certain I cross'd this place, heard the relief go round, & thought to have Takun the century; but he fired on us. I remained here Till day breake, when I returned at the beating of the revillee To this place. I must cross the Bridge to get some refreshment for the Troops, & particularly our Horses are almost Starved, & nothing but grass in the woods to be got. Should the enemy move I shall continue to follow them & give You the very best

---

[27] Maj. Genl. Gates to Lt. Col. Porterfield, 8 August, 1780, in "Horatio Gates, Major General, Commanding Southern Army. Letters and Orders from June 21st to August 31st, 1780", in *Magazine of American History, Vol. 5, No. 4,* (October, 1880), 300

information possible. All their Waggons left this early yesterday & I expect they intend marching this day for Camden, alth' they have given out they intend to make a Stand where they now are. "[28]

The force that Porterfield observed was commanded by Lord Rawdon, a competent and experienced officer. It included elements of the 23rd, 33rd, and 71st regiments, as well as the Volunteers of Ireland, forty dragoons, and four cannon.[29] They held a strong position on the south bank of Little Lynches Creek and were far too formidable for Porterfield to attack.

General Gates apparently expressed some concern that Porterfield was at risk, because the colonel wrote a second letter to alleviate the General's concern.

"I acknowledge the recp't of Your favour, & the wagons are come up here, but I believe perfectly secure, as I am determined To dispute to the last the passage of Lynche's Bridge.

To make sure my conjectures concerning the British army moving this morning, I went with some of the Horse and foot to reconnoiter their camp...I advanced to their Retreat and fired on them. Sevral shot were exchanged so as to alarm them To parade their Troops, which lay so situated that it was impossible to injure them with my force.

I send You a prisoner Tooke by our Retreat...Their whole core marched To the Bridge, & had we known anything of their coming would fell into our own hands; but takeing them for a party

---

[28] Lt. Col. Charles Porterfield to Gen. Gates, in *The State Records of North Carolina 1779-1780, Vol. 14*, 546

[29] Lieut. Col. H. L. Landers, F. A., *The Battle of Camden, South Carolina: August 16, 1780*, (U.S. Govt. Printing Office: Washington, 1929), 18-19

from the enemy's camp, our scouts fired on them, which alarmed them & prevented their falling Timely into our hands, which they would have done. This minute we have four more, & expect more Yet."[30]

Early the next morning, General Gates marched his army towards Porterfield's position. Anticipating battle, he ordered that,

"The Whole Army is to be held in Readiness to parade at the Shortest Notice. The Troops will constantly assemble their Alarm Posts in Front of their respective Brigades at the beating of Reveille and upon every alarm. The General hopes to find his Officers and Men alert, and always prepared for Action."[31]

Sometime in the evening of August 10th, however, General Gates concluded that the enemy's position was too strong to assault. He decided to bypass it by marching up the north bank of Little Lynches Creek. Gates ordered the cavalry and infantry, under Armand and Porterfield, to protect the army's rear during the march.[32] The march continued the next day with Armand's cavalry returning to the van and Porterfield's infantry covering the left flank of the army.[33] General Gates halted at Rudgely's Mill on August 13th, thirteen miles north

---

[30] Lieut. Col. Porterfield to Gen. Gates, 9 August, 1780, in *The State Records of North Carolina 1779-1780, Vol. 14,* 547
[31] After General Orders for August 10, 1780, in "Horatio Gates, Major General, Commanding Southern Army. Letters and Orders from June 21st to August 31st, 1780", in *Magazine of American History, Vol. 5, No. 4,* (October, 1880), 318
[32] Ibid. (General Orders for August 11, 1780)
[33] Ibid. (General Orders for August 12, 1780)

of Camden. Colonel Porterfield's infantry was placed in front again, across a nearby creek on the road to Camden.[34]

The American maneuver forced Lord Rawdon to abandon his position and withdraw to the outskirts of Camden to protect that valuable post. Four companies of British light infantry, from the garrison at Ninety-Six, reinforced Rawdon. Another important re-enforcement arrived in the form of General Cornwallis, who, on August 13th, assumed overall command at Camden.[35] The Americans received their own re-enforcements when 700 Virginia militia arrived under General Edward Stevens.

Colonel Porterfield, concerned with the dwindling number of North Carolina militia in his corps, requested that some of the newly arrived Virginians be attached to him.

> *"I have not more than eighty of the* [North Carolina] *militia now with me & I expect some of them will desert this day. I met five on their way as I came down. I wish more officers and men could be sent from the Virginians."*[36]

General Gates complied with Porterfield's request and issued the necessary orders the next day.

---

[34] Banastre Tarleton, *A History of the Campaigns of 1780 and 1781 in the Southern Provinces of North America*, (reprinted in NY: Arno Press, 1968), 102

[35] Ibid.

[36] Col Porterfield to Maj. Genl. Gates, in *The State Records of North Carolina 1779-1780, Vol. 14*, 558

"Gen. Stevens will immediately order one Captain, two Lieutenants, one Ensign, three Sergeants, one Drum and sixty Rank and File to join Col. Porterfield's Infantry. These men are to be taken from the most experienced woodsmen every way fitted for the Service."[37]

Re-enforced to nearly 400 men, Colonel Porterfield prepared for action.[38]

---

[37] General Orders for August 15, 1780, in "Horatio Gates, Major General, Commanding Southern Army. Letters and Orders from June 21st to August 31st, 1780", in *Magazine of American History, Vol. 5, No. 4,* (October, 1880), 320

[38] Landers, 40

Southern Theater

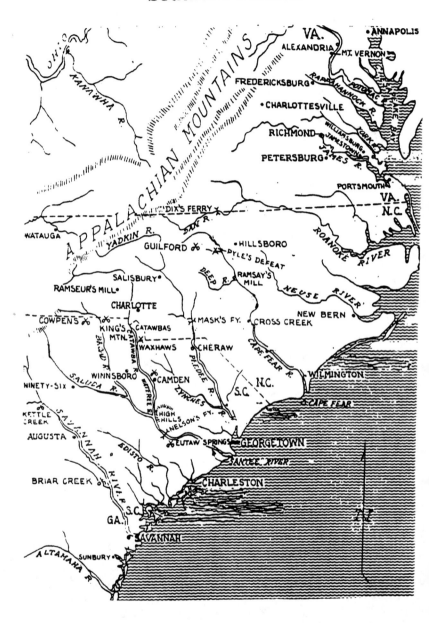

Chapter Eight

The Battle of Camden

On August 14th, Lieutenant Colonel Senf, an engineer, and Lieutenant Colonel Porterfield, was sent ahead of the American army to locate a strong, defensible, position closer to Camden. By establishing such a post on the outskirts of Camden, Gates hoped to restrict the enemy's operations in the area, sever some of their supply routes, and harass them with light detachments. Eventually, such activity would compel the British to either abandon Camden or attack the fortified American position.[1]

The two officers returned on August 15th.

> "[They] *reported that they had found a position 5 or 6 miles in advance, with a thick swamp on the right, a deep creek in front & thick low ground on the left…"*[2]

General Gates, eager to occupy the ground, prepared the army for a night march. His marching orders were clear.

> *"The Troops will be ready to march precisely at 10 o'clock in the following order – viz. Colonel Armands Cavalry commanded by Colonel Armand—Colonel Porterfield's Lt Infry upon the Right Flank of Colonel Armand in Indian File, Two Hundred Yards from the Road—Major Armstrong's Light infantry in the Same Order of Colonel Porterfield's upon the left Flank of*

---

[1] Thomas Pinckney to William Johnson, 27 July, 1822 in *Historical Magazine*, Vol. 10 No. 8 (Aug. 1886), 244
(Accessed via the Documentary History of the Battle of Camden website at http://battleofcamden.org)
[2] Ibid.

the Legion...[The rest of the army would follow the advance guard] *In this Order the Troops will proceed and thus March this night. In case you attack the Enemy's Cavalry in Front, the Light Infantry upon each Flank, will instantly march up, and give and Continue the most galling Fire upon the Enemy's Horse – this will enable Colonel Armand not only to support the Shock of the Enemy's Charge, but finally to rout them...The Troops will observe the profoundest Silence upon the March, and any Soldier who offers to fire without the Command of his officers must be instantly put to death.*"[3]

The American army was on the move and Colonel Porterfield, like he had done numerous times before, commanded the advance guard. Porterfield accompanied the right wing of the guard. It consisted of the remnants of his state detachment and the "picked" militiamen from General Stevens newly arrived brigade. They marched Indian file (one single line), paralleling the road (and Armand's cavalry). The remnants of the North Carolina light troops comprised the left wing of the guard. They also paralleled Armand's cavalry. Armand sent a videt about 300 yards in advance of the guard. The infantry was originally ordered to march 200 yards off the road, but for reasons unknown, they were only 25 yards from it.[4]

[3] Otho Williams, "A Narrative of the Campaign of 1781" in William Johnson, *Sketches of the Life and Correspondence of Nathaniel Greene, Vol. 1,* (Charleston: A.E. Miller, 1822), 492-493 (Accessed via the Documentary History of the Battle of Camden website at http://battleofcamden.org)
[4] Guilford Dudley, "A Sketch of the Military Services Performed by Guilford Dudley, Then of the Town of Halifax, North Carolina, During the Revolutionary War", Charles Campbell, ed. *Southern Literary Messenger,* Vol. 11, Issues 3-6 (1845), 146 (Accessed via http://battleofcamden.org)

Riding with Colonel Porterfield was twenty four year old Guilford Dudley, of Halifax, North Carolina. Dudley's account of the opening engagement at Camden is one of the finest first person narratives of the Revolutionary War.

"At length the fatal night of the 15th of August, 1780 arrived, when Gates, precisely at 10 o'clock...put his army in motion—the light troops moving simultaneously, joined ...by 200 exhausted raw Virginia militia, and Col. Armand's corps of dragoons, consisting of about 60 privates marching in order of battle after the following disposition: the foot divided into two bodies, moved by files through the open piney woods plain, 25 yards out of the great Waxhaw road; the right flank headed by Col. Porterfield (commandant of the whole corps in person,) whilst Capt. Drew with his Virginia regulars, (about 55, and mostly raw levies,) composed the leading company of that flank. The left flank of infantry, under the care of Major Armstrong, moved in like order...Col. Armand, with his dragoons in column, occupied the road which was here a dead level and very spacious.

It became my duty by direction to post myself on the right side of Colonel Porterfield, as he had on several occasions before, made use of me (a private soldier) to carry his orders to other officers of his command, and in one or two instances, to repair to the main army on business. In this order we slowly advanced, to give time to the main army to approximate us in the most profound silence; it being expressly stated in Gen. Gates's last orders, that any person speaking above his breath, should be instantly put to death on the spot where the violation occurred.

Lord Cornwallis, as it was afterwards ascertained, by a singular coincidence, put his army in motion at the same hour in the night that Gates moved, to strike him in his camp at Clermont the next morning at the break of day, while Gates's object was to move down upon Camden at night. The consequence of this simultaneous movement of both armies was, that we met about half way near Sutton's plantation between 12 and 1 o'clock in the night. The moon was at full and shone beautifully; not a breath of air was stirring, nor a cloud to be seen big as a man's hand. Consequently, we could see to fight in the open piney wood plains, destitute of brush wood almost, as well in the night as in the day.

Tarleton, with his dragoons, (said to be 350,) with a suitable number of infantry, composed the British van. Armand's videt, who rode about 300 yards in our front, decried the enemy advancing upon him, and at that instant emptied his pistol, and came clattering in with all the speed his horse could make. The discharge of the pistol was most distinctly heard through all the American corps.

A pause ensued, when Col. Armand, in the road...put spurs to his horse, and at full speed dashed from the road to the front of our right flank of infantry; and leaning over his saddle, in an audible whisper said to Col. Porterfield, 'there is the enemy, Sir – must I charge him.' Porterfield, who was a serious man, of few words, and slow of speech, gravely replied in the tone of Armand, 'by all means, Sir.' I was at this moment...riding on the right side of the American commandant...and distinctly heard Armand's communication and the question it involved, together with the reply, although all was expressed only in a whisper.

Armand, instantly wheeling his horse, rushed on to the head of his column, which he had left but a few seconds before, when Tarleton, sounding a charge,

128

came on at the top of his speed, every officer and soldier with the yell of an Indian savage – at every leap their horses took, crying out, 'charge, charge, charge,' so that their own voices and the echoes resounded in every direction through the pine forest."[5]

Dudley noted that most of the militia, along with Armand's cavalry, broke to the rear upon Tarleton's charge. Colonel Armand and his front troops held firm, however, meeting the enemy with pistols and sabers. The cavalry clash spurred Porterfield into action. Dudley's account continues.

"Col. Porterfield, now breaking silence, as soon as he heard the enemy's clamor, and saw their swift approach towards the front of Armand's column, with his usual composure and deliberate manner, ordered his right flank of infantry to 'advance,' which order was hastily executed in a step approaching to a trot, keeping our due distance from the road, and in a line parallel to it, when pretty well covering Tarleton's left flank, though we were far from seeing to its rear, by reason of the great length of his column. Porterfield ordered, 'halt, face to the road and fire.' This order was executed with the velocity of a flash of lightning, spreading from right to left, and again the piney forest resounded with the thunder of our musketry; whilst the astonished British dragoons, looking only straight before them along the road, counting no doubt with certainty upon extirpating Armand's handful of cavalry, and not dreaming that they were flanked on the right and on the left by our infantry, within point-blank shot, drew up, wheeled their horses, and retreating with the

[5] Ibid. 146-147

utmost precipitation, were out of our reach before we could possibly ram down another cartridge...

No sooner had Tarleton received one destructive fire on his right and on his left, and retreated out of our reach, than the British infantry, who were close at hand, advanced in column to the number, it was said, of about 500, but which, probably, did not exceed 350. Porterfield, holding up his fire until he saw his enemy between our two flanks of infantry, commenced his fire at close distance, which was answered by our left flank, under Capt. Lockhart, with equal spirit and deliberation.

The enemy seemed for an instant to pause, but conscious of their superiority in numbers as well as discipline, facing to their right and left, returned upon us a heavy fire, which enveloped us from our right to left, in consequence of the recession of so large a number of troops in the commencement of the action, leaving us only 100 or less on both flanks to contend with the unbroken, undismayed column of the enemy; but soon the remains of our left flank, under Capt. Lockhart, receded also, and hastily falling back in an oblique direction from the road, formed on the extreme of the left wing of our army, now forming, and composed of Stephen's brigade of Virginia militia...The conflict on our right, where Porterfield in person commanded, became, therefore, more unequal and destructive; yet Porterfield maintained his ground with great firmness and gallantry for about five rounds, with this handful of men, not more than 50 at this time.

The enemy, without leaving the road and advancing upon us as he might have done, pushed his column along until he passed our left, when giving us a cross-fire from both his flanks, as well as from his centre directly in our front, he threatened instant extermination to our brave little band. At length both sides being simultaneously prepared, poured in upon each other the heaviest fire that had been yet exchanged during the conflict. At this fire, Porterfield with horse's head reined directly to the enemy, received a horrid wound in his left leg, a little before the knee, which shattered it to pieces, when falling forward upon the pommel of his saddle, he directed Captain Drew, who was close by his side, to order a retreat, which was done in a very deliberate tone of voice by the Captain, and instantly our little band retreated obliquely from the road, which was wholly secluded from us by the enemy. At this moment I was ten or twelve yards down the line from the Colonel with my horse's...nose touching the shoulders of our rear rank.

Glancing my eye from left to right as the enemy poured his fire, I fixed it upon Porterfield at the instant he received the ball and fell upon the pommel of his saddle, when wheeling my horse I dashed up to the Colonel, while Drew having given the order for retreat, was on his left side, in the act of wheeling his horse from the enemy, with the intent to carry him off. Locking my left arm in the Colonel's right to support him in the saddle on that side, and having completely turned his horse, we received another hot fire from the enemy directed solely upon us at the distance of thirty yards or less. Upon this the Colonel's horse, very docile and standing fire with the same steady composure as his master, having no doubt been grazed by a ball which he sensibly felt, reared, plunged forward and dropt his rider on the spot, who had a severe fall in his maimed condition, and had liked to have dragged me off my horse with our arms locked, and the horse going off with his accoutrements at the top of his speed, followed the track of the retreating soldiers.

At the very instant Porterfield's horse reared and plunged forward, Captain Drew fell prostrate on his face, and that to naturally, that I entertained no doubt but he was killed. The Captain, however, receiving no injury, and being an active, nimble little man, was presently on his feet, and wheeling around the stern of my horse, was in a moment out of sight. Thus left entirely alone with the Colonel, who was flat upon the ground with his head towards the enemy and his shattered leg doubled under him, entreating me not to leave him, I sprang from my horse and seizing him with an Indian hug around the waist, by a sudden effort jerked him up upon his well leg.

Then again the Colonel, in the most pathetic manner, apparently dreading instant death, brave as he was, or captivity, entreated me, as he had done before, not to forsake him; the blood, in the meantime gushing out of his wound in a torrent as big as a large straw or goose-quill, which presently overflowed the top of his large, loose boot and dyed the ground all around him. Pale as a piece of bleached linen, and ready to faint with the loss of blood and the anguish of his wound, he made another appeal to my feelings in the manner above described, from an apprehension, as I then believed, that I would not have firmness enough to stand by him under the trying circumstances... when I replied the second time, as I had in the first instance, with much earnestness and energy, 'that I would carry him off or perish with him.'

Upon this assurance, twice repeated, the Colonel became tranquillized and seemed patiently to wait his doom, which he expected would be nothing less than instant death or captivity, the latter of which, at that *moment, in his miserable situation, I believe to have been as appalling to his mind as the first. While we stood thus in front of the enemy, with my horse uncommonly gentle and no ways alarmed at the firing, drawn up close by my side, we received another fire from a platoon of the enemy just in our front, whilst the rest of their line seemed to have slackened theirs, and in no wise annoyed us.*

Still clasping Colonel Porterfield in my arms and supporting him upon his well leg, his back to the enemy, my face and right shoulder above his left, looking intently at the enemy to see if a file or section would leave the road and advance upon us with charged bayonets, I made three violent essays to throw him upon my horse, which was tall, and thus endeavor to carry him off.

My efforts were perfectly fruitless. I was then young and light, and Colonel Porterfield was a man of the largest size, perhaps 6 feet and an inch or two in height, round limbed and fleshy, but not corpulent, although he weighed perhaps 210 pounds and was about 30 or 32 years of age. Although I several times poised him and raised him a little from the ground, yet as he could only stand upon one leg with my support, the other dangling from side to side and sometimes behind as I moved him, and incapable of bounding in the least from the earth, I was incapable with my utmost exertions of throwing him into my saddle.

In this dilemma I ceased to make any further efforts to throw him upon my horse and resolved calmly to wait the result whatever it might be, nor did Porterfield attempt to give me any direction in this emergency, or express an opinion how I ought to act for his relief or my own preservation, but appeared to be entirely resigned to whatever fate might await him

133

in his exhausted and fainting condition. Still holding up the Colonel upon his well leg, watching the motions of the enemy and not unfrequently turning my head over either shoulder, casting a wishful and exploring eye on every side and in the rear, to see if no friendly assistance could be obtained, however improbable, (for all was silence; not a living soul to be seen but the enemy in the road, occasionally giving us a scattering but ineffectual fire.)

I was at last so fortunate as to fix my eyes upon two men at the distance of about 150 yards in my rear, running back with great speed, half bent and with trailed arms, towards where they supposed the main body, under Gates, was by this time halted. Although I could not at the moment divine where these men came from, I yet, nevertheless, with joy as well as surprise recognized them for American troops by their garb, their manner and by their clumsy wooden canteens slung over their shoulders upon their blankets and knapsacks, all which I could plainly discover by the brilliant light of the moon, casting her beams with great lustre over the open piney wood plain.

Believing this providential discovery would be the last resource I should be favored with to save Porterfield and myself, I was determined to avail myself of it if possible at every risk, and therefore endeavoring somewhat to modulate the tone of my voice, with great eagerness I called out to them, "come here, come here," without saying for what purpose or mentioning any names.

Whether they had seen us before or not I cannot say, but hearing my voice, they instantly turned their heads in the direction where Porterfield and myself stood, though without slackening their pace, and kept on with rather increased speed and bodies lower bent ...Seeing them no ways disposed to come at my call to our assistance, and knowing that we should be lost without it, I resolved to make one desperate effort to draw them to us before they should get out of my sight or hearing. I therefore in a very loud tone of voice and with much energy, regardless of the immediate proximity of the enemy, cried out, 'by G-d, come and help me away with Colonel Porterfield.'

This name, pronounced with so much emphasis, operated on the feelings of these two honest young soldiers like magic, and they instantly wheeled and came running to us with all their speed, no longer half bent to conceal themselves among the wire-grass, but with erect countenance and a determined air.[6]

One of these men was John Gibson of Louisa County, Virginia. He was a private in the Virginia militia and recalled helping Colonel Porterfield years later in his pension application.

"They [Porterfield's Corps] *marched within twenty steps of the enemy and were fired on, returned the fire and after firing twice were ordered to retreat and oblique to the right. He marched a few steps and found Col. Porterfield down and his horse dead on him, assisted in getting him out and putting him on a horse and then in bearing him off the field. He carried him a few hundred yards and then he cut off the boot from his broken leg."*[7]

---

[6] Ibid. 147-148, 231-232

[7] Pension Application of John Gibson, in *Virginia Revolutionary Pension Applications, Vol. 43*, Abstracted & Compiled by John Frederick Dorman, (Washington, D.C., 1991), 37

Guilford Dudley's account provides much more detail of Colonel Porterfield's rescue.

"No sooner had they [the two soldiers] *reached us and laid down their muskets and fixed bayonets by my direction, than they seized Porterfield by both his arms and around his body to sustain him in the position they found him in upon coming up. Then I sprang into my saddle and ordered them to lift him up carefully over the stern of my horse and place him close to the hind tree of my saddle, (the Colonel instantly clinging to me with both arms around my waist,) and then directing them to resume their muskets with one hand and each with the other to sustain him in his seat across the loins of the horse, taking care to steady his shattered leg so as to keep it from swinging about under the flanks of the horse, and to prevent his falling off behind.*

All these instructions were obeyed with an alacrity and cheerfulness that instantly won my affections and confidence; and thus fixed, with the reins of the bridle in my own hand, I moved slowly off in a direction perpendicular to the road, not daring to oblique to my right or march parallel to the road to gain our main body, lest I should be intercepted by the enemy, who had pushed the front sections or files of their light infantry along up the Waxhaw road, for some distance beyond the spot where we had fought, and gave us all in a group as we were, a scattering, parting fire, with no more effect than if it had been made with little boy's pop-guns...so wretchedly did they take aim, as I had discovered from the first fire at the commencement of the action, for at the distance of only 25 yards from the road many of their balls whizzed along six feet above our heads, while others struck the ground before they reached us, and rebounding passed off without doing much injury that I could perceive, whilst others that were better directed produced, as might be supposed, the most destructive effects, the lamented Porterfield being one instance.

But to resume: thus fixed, with the Colonel clinging around my waist, we marched very slowly off to save him all the pain we possibly could in his melancholy situation. We had, however, scarcely progressed more than 30 or 40 yards before he fainted with loss of blood and the anguish of his wound, and was very nearly falling off backwards over the stern of my horse, but was sustained in his seat by my two faithful companions.

We were then compelled to halt, although still in sight of the enemy, to give the Colonel time to breathe a little, I ordering the soldiers to dash some water they fortunately had in their awkward wooden canteens in his face, when, clasping his arms around my waist the second time, for he had unconsciously unlocked his hands when he first fainted, we moved quietly off again, but had scarcely proceeded more than 40 yards further when he fainted the second time, but was soon revived by the use of the same means as were first applied.

He then, in the most pathetic and moving accents, entreated me to lay him down and let him abide his fate. whatever it might prove; but this I refused, and exhorted him with all the energy and force of reasoning that I was master of, to bear his miserable situation a little longer and he should be safe, telling him that the enemy was yet still in view, although he did not pursue at that moment; yet in all probability, nay, to a certainty, his discomfited cavalry would, in a few minutes, return and scour the whole plain in our front, rear and all around us, when we should all be inevitably lost.

Yielding to these arguments, the Colonel became passive, and then directing my companions to hold him fast in his present seat, (finding there was great danger of his falling off as he became more exhausted,) I sprang from my saddle upon the ground and joining with them, directed them to assist me to lift the Colonel over the hind-tree into the seat of the saddle that I had just left, and then springing up myself behind him and clasping my arms around his waist, I directed one of the men to take the reins of the bridle and guide the horse himself, as I could no longer do it in my changed position, both my hands and arms being employed in this manner. With the same alacrity as they had manifested upon all occasions before, my order was obeyed, and thus we moved on the third time as before.

But unfortunately, although the Colonel's new position was more safe and easy than before, yet, nevertheless, growing more weak and exhausted every moment, he presently fainted the third and then the fourth time, while I pressed him around the body with both my arms and sustained him in his seat without his saying another word or entreating to be laid down as he had done before. But in both these last cases he revived by the free use of the contents of the wooden canteens, which contained nothing but warm, dead water, only drinkable from necessity.

Most fortunately, at the last instance of his fainting, we were emerging into a little thicket of small persimmon bushes, about waist high...At first it had been impracticable to place a bandage around his leg, as we had neither time nor means to accomplish it, though it would evidently be attended with advantage to the unfortunate Colonel, but there *was no brush-wood or other growth from which a handful of twigs could be cut for the purpose of splintering his leg before the bandage was applied.*

No sooner, therefore, did I cast my eye over the aforesaid cluster of little persimmon shrubs, than the idea of availing myself of their use occurred. And directing the soldier who had the bridle-rein in his hand and was guiding the horse to halt, I slipped off from behind Porterfield and requested him to tear off a bandage from one side of his blanket its whole length, whilst I should, pulling out my pocket knife for the purpose, cut a bundle of twigs 10 or 12 inches in length and hastily trim them to apply all around the Colonel's leg before the bandage was wrapped over them. This request was also instantly complied with, and the bundle of pliant twigs being expeditiously prepared with the assistance of this soldier, whilst the other held Porterfield fast in the saddle, I very soon bound up his leg in many folds of the strip of blanket as tight as I could draw it, which almost entirely stanched the blood, and then resuming my seat behind him we soon moved on again for the last time, steering our course as before, due West as near as possible.

This surgical-like operation was of infinite, advantage to Porterfield, who no more fainted or complained. And thus we moved on without any further interruption or delay, perhaps a mile and a half from the road where we fought, when we were stopped by one of those large, flat, impassable morasses, that so frequently occur in the pine plains of South Carolina...Here, of necessity, we were obliged to halt, and fortunately striking the margin of the morass, where grew a large laurel sapling with its dark green and glossy leaves just in the edge of the marsh, with a wide spreading bushy top which cast a deep shade upon the ground eastward, I determined to lay the exhausted Colonel down, and stretching him at full length in the shade of the laurel with his leg and thigh bolstered up with my great-coat which was fastened to the pomel of my saddle, and taking time to tie my horse to a limb of the same laurel with his fore feet in the water and mud to conceal him as much as possible in the dark shade of the sappling, as well as Porterfield and myself, resolving to remain alone by Porterfield's side, I sent off my two faithful companions, with directions to search for Gates' army, where or at what distance we knew not; nor did Porterfield offer a conjecture on the subject, or give a single order from first to last respecting the premises, seeing that every thing was done by ardent friends that mortal man under existing circumstances could accomplish for his relief and safety.

The order I gave them was, upon finding the army, to bring up two or three surgeons and as many men as would afford a relief or two to bear off the Colonel on a litter. No sooner did I deliver this request, than these two willing, generous soldiers, with their arms in their bands and their knapsacks and canteens slung upon their backs, departed almost in a run to execute the order just received, upon the speedy execution of which depended the life of the Colonel as well as my own.

Porterfield was lying in the shade of the laurel on the edge of the morass with his feet towards Camden. I laid my unsheathed sabre and pistols on the ground by his side and within a few feet of my horse. It now being two hours before day-break, I laid myself down along-side of the Colonel, feeling weary after fatiguing marches in the hot season. Thus prostrate on the earth, Porterfield being indisposed to talking from natural taciturnity and from exhaustion, a painful silence ensued, which however, was sometimes interrupted first, by our own light-horse in full gallop sweeping along the plain within thirty or forty yards of the spot where we lay close to the ground in the shade of the laurel, and then bearing to their left further off the morass into the plain 'till we lost sight of them and then the British dragoons, who were all in motion, coming in the other direction and scampering over the plain, sometimes at a considerable distance, but the tread of whose horses' feet lying as we were, flat on the ground, we could distinctly hear as well as the confused voices of their riders, patrolling in every direction. On these occasions, Porterfield, in a feeble voice, would make some remarks as well as myself, but finding from the direction they took as I reported it to him, (for he never raised his head,) that they would not be upon us, he sank again into a state of silence and apathy.

At last a large patrol of British dragoons came from the South in the direction of Camden, and in a brisk gallop came on pressing close in upon the margin of the swamp, coming apparently, directly upon us, when, as before, I was aroused first by the trampling of their horses and then by a full view of them, after raising myself up upon my left elbow, at the distance of thirty or forty yards, when seizing my pistols, I hastily cocked one and was about to stand upright, but Porterfield, who now expected we should be discovered and consequently lost, feebly stretched out his right arm and laying his hand on mine, entreated that I would not fire, alleging that if I did they would cut us to pieces without mercy; for being in a desperate situation, and feeling no inclination to fall into their hand and trust to the clemency of British dragoons, I had resolved to sell my life as dear as possible, and after emptying both my pistols, to resume my sabre and defend myself to the last extremity as long as possible, announcing, however, at the same time, the name of Porterfield and asking quarter for him, and then with my arms in hand, leaving my horse behind, plunge into the morass and scramble over as well as I could, knowing that further pursuit was impracticable.

These resolves were formed with the rapidity of thought, and the execution of them would have been attempted as far as practicable, but fortunately, the same kind Providence who had so wonderfully protected and shielded us during the various past scenes of the night after Porterfield was wounded, did not forsake us now; for almost in the same instant that I descried them, they bore away to their right and I presently lost sight of them among the lofty pine trees of the forest.

This was the last patrol that made its appearance on either side, and as soon as we felt safe from further search, we sank down in our sleepless repose. In fifteen or twenty minutes after this last occurrence, as the Colonel and myself were lying in profound silence and the day beginning to break, we heard most distinctly the report of a cannon, fired in the direction of Camden, which echoed through the plains at the distance of six miles, when asking the Colonel the meaning of it, he informed me in a feeble voice, that it was their morning gun...This was not only a morning gun fired to awaken the garrison, but was also designed, as I believed to serve as a signal for Lord Cornwallis to put his army in motion and prepare for the battle just at hand, both armies having formed in the night and lain on their arms within two hundred and fifty yards of each other.

Just at this crisis, at break of day, my two faithful companions returned, bringing with them three or four surgeons, one of which was the surgeon of the Halifax volunteers; the rest were of the Maryland line, together with Capt. Drew, Lieut. Vaughn, Ensign V___, and eight privates of Drew's company. and several more, who, hearing of Porterfield's situation and the place where he lay, followed after them. The surgeons immediately fell to work upon the Colonel, but did nothing more than to take off my bandage and twig splinters and put on their own boards and bandages, whilst the rest of us were busily engaged in cutting down small pile saplings of which to form a litter to carry him off. These things were speedily accomplished, the Colonel was carefully placed on the litter, which was raised up from the ground and placed on the shoulders of four men, when the procession began to move off in solemn silence.

The dawn of day then appearing, I stepped back a few paces and putting up my arms and mounting my horse, accompanied them thirty or forty yards in the direction they were going, when suddenly the stillness of the dawn was startled by one of our parks of artillery, which at once served as a signal for battle and as a guide to direct me to the spot where our army was formed... Upon this firing, the meaning of which I was at no loss to understand, I wheeled my horse and riding back a few paces to the side of the litter, took an affectionate farewell of Colonel Porterfield, telling him at the same time, that I hoped to join him again in the course of an hour or two, which was in sincerity my expectation, so sanguine were my hopes of immediate victory, notwithstanding the disasters of the past night. Vain hope! I never more set my eyes on Porterfield, for here we parted

143

— I steering my course to the army by the roar of our cannon, and the rest of the company, with the surgeons, falling back northwardly and shaping their course in a direction where they hoped to find some plantation at which to leave the Colonel with the necessary attendants, until the battle should be over.[8]

The early morning collision between the two advance parties surprised General Gates and created some disorder in the American ranks. Fortunately, the British did not press the attack and the Americans were able to reform. However, with British troops already across Saunders Creek, the American plan to fortify the area had to be scrapped.

General Gates assembled a war council to determine his next move. Colonel Otho Williams described the meeting.

"All the general officers immediately assembled in the rear of the line: the unwelcome news was communicated to them. General Gates said, 'Gentlemen, what is to be done?' All were mute for a few moments – when the gallant Stevens exclaimed, 'Gentlemen, is it not too late now to do any thing but fight?' No other advice was offered, and the general desired the gentlemen would repair to their respective commands."[9]

The American army formed for battle. The 2nd Maryland brigade and the Delaware regiment held the right side of the road. Their right flank was protected by an impassable swamp. The North Carolina militia held the center, connecting with the Delaware regiment on their right and the Virginia militia on their left.

---

[8] Dudley, 232-235
[9] Williams, 494-495

Battle of Camden

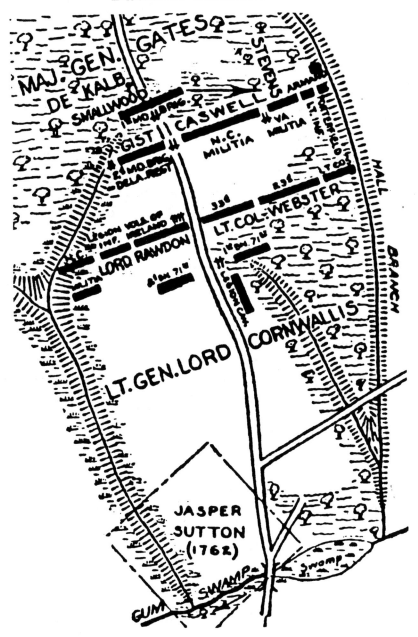

The remnants of Porterfield's corps and Armand's cavalry held the extreme left of the American line. Their left flank was also protected by a swamp. The Americans had roughly 3,300 men, but two thirds were inexperienced militia.[10] Although the British had fewer troops, roughly 2,000, most were battle tested veterans, commanded by Britain's best general, Lord Cornwallis. The battle commenced at dawn with an American cannonade of the British, who were only two hundred yards away. General Gates, informed that the enemy was in the midst of forming their line and vulnerable to attack, ordered General Stevens to advance his brigade of Virginia militia. By the time the Virginians complied, however, the British had formed their line and the opportunity was lost. Undeterred, Colonel Otho Williams, *"requested General Stevens to let him have forty or fifty privates, volunteers, who would commence the attack."*[11] Colonel Williams described what happened.

> *"They were led forward within forty or fifty yards of the enemy, and ordered to take trees and keep up as brisk a fire as possible. The desired effect of this expedient, to extort the enemy's fire at some distance in order to the rendering it less terrible to the militia, was not gained. General Stevens, observing the enemy to rush on, put his men in mind of their bayonets..."*[12]

General Stevens gave a similar, albeit less detailed account of the action to Governor Jefferson four days after the battle.

---

[10] Landers, 45
[11] Williams, 495
[12] Ibid.

"...We formed and remained on the ground till about day Break when we advanced a few Hundred Yards and fell in with each other...our left where I was had gained such an Advantage over the Enemy in outflanking their Right; but alas on the first Fire or two they Charged and the Militia gave way..."[13]

Garret Watts, one of the volunteers with Colonel Williams, gave a much more detailed and personal account of the militia's conduct.

"I remember that I was among the nearest to the enemy;...that we had orders to wait for the word to commence firing; that the militia were in front and in a feeble condition at that time. They were fatigued. The weather was warm excessively. They had been fed a short time previously on molasses entirely. I can state on oath that I believe my gun was the first gun fired, notwithstanding the orders, for we were close to the enemy, who appeared to maneuver in contempt of us, and I fired without thinking except that I might prevent the man opposite from killing me. The discharge and loud roar soon became general from one end of the line to the other. Amongst other things, I confess I was amongst the first that fled. The cause of that I cannot tell, except that everyone I saw was about to do the same. It was instantaneous. There was no effort to rally, no encouragement to fight. Officers and men joined in the flight. I threw away my gun, and reflecting I might be punished for being found without arms, I picked up a drum, which gave forth such sounds when touched by twigs I cast it away. When we had

---

[13] General Edward Stevens to Governor Jefferson, 20 August, 1780, in *The Papers of Thomas Jefferson, Vol. 3, 558*

gone, we heard the roar of guns still, but we knew not why. Had we known, we might have returned. It was that portion of the army commanded by de Kalb fighting still."[14]

As the roar of guns suggested, the situation on the American right wing was much different. William Seymour, a soldier in the Delaware regiment, described the engagement there.

"We advanced...and began the attack from both cannon and small arms with great alacrity and uncommon bravery, making great havock among them, insomuch that the enemy gave way... "[15]

Otho Williams also described the fight on the American right.

"The Second Maryland Brigade, including the battalion of Delawares, on the right, were engaged with the enemy's left, which they opposed with very great firmness. They even advanced upon them and had taken a number of prisoners... "[16]

While General De Kalb's men held firm on the right, the American left was in disarray. The rout of the militia troops seriously weakened the American army (by nearly two thirds). General Smallwood's 1st Maryland brigade (the reserve) advanced in an effort to hold the left flank. They engaged the enemy in a ferocious fight. Outnumbered and outflanked,

[14] Garret Watts Pension Statement, Revolutionary Pension Roll, in Vol. 14 Sen. Doc. 514, 23rd Cong., 1st sess., 1833-34
(Accessed via the Documentary History of the Battle of Camden website at http://battleofcamden.org)
[15] William Seymour, "Journal of the Southern Expedition, 1780-1783", in *The Pennsylvania Magazine of History and Biography, Vol. 7*, (1883), 288
[16] Williams, 496

however, they were soon forced to give ground. Attempts to counterattack and join General De Kalb's continentals, who were two hundred yards to their right, failed.[17]

The British exploited the gap between the two Maryland brigades, driving through it and into the rear of the 2nd Maryland. Other British forces turned the left flank of the 1st Maryland brigade. De Kalb's continentals were nearly surrounded and the general, seriously wounded. Colonel Williams described the end.

> *"The enemy having collected their corps and directing their whole force against these two devoted brigades, a tremendous fire of musketry was for some time kept up on both sides with equal perseverance and obstinacy, until Lord Cornwallis, perceiving there was no cavalry opposed to him, pushed forward his dragoons, and his infantry charging at the same moment with fixed bayonets put an end to the contest. His victory was complete. All the artillery and a very great number of prisoners fell into his hands. Many fine fellows lay on the field, and the rout of the remainder was entire. Not even a company retired in any order. Every one escaped as he could."*[18]

General De Kalb, who held his position to the end, lay mortally wounded upon the field. The bodies of his men lay all around him. Total American losses were estimated at over 1,000 (250 killed and 800 wounded and/or captured). The British lost only one third that number.[19]

Once again, an American army was smashed by the British in South Carolina. Once again, resistance to the British in South Carolina was left to assorted militia and irregular units.

---

[17] Landers, 48
[18] Williams, 496
[19] Buchanan, 170

General Gates, who was swept up in the initial retreat of the militia, halted in North Carolina and commenced the difficult task of rebuilding his fractured army. He undoubtedly hoped to redeem his reputation by returning to the field. He never got that chance, however. It was left to his successor, General Nathaniel Greene, to re-establish continental resistance in the south.

Such resistance occurred without the participation of Colonel Charles Porterfield. Abandoned by the routed American army, he was captured in a house near Rudgley Mills. His shattered leg made escape impossible. Four days after his capture, he wrote to General Gates for assistance.

> *"Sir: I am now at this place a prisoner of war on parole, with one of my legs quite broke by a musket ball, & without any surgeon to attend me. I have been here since Wednesday last, being only once visited by a surgeon from the Maryland line, a prisoner.*
>
> *The British officers at Rudgesley's have treated me with the utmost attention & politeness, & have furnished me with such necessaries as in their power; also have wrote to Camden in my behalf, but such is the situation of affairs that I expect no surgeon can be spared.*
>
> *As my life in this season depends on speedy relief, I have to pray a surgeon skilled be sent To attend for some Time. This, I hope, will be granted, as every indulgence seems to be the wish of those under whose direction I am."*[20]

Word spread within the American army that Lieutenant Colonel Porterfield had suffered a mortal wound. Some

---

[20] Lt. Col. Porterfield to General Gates, 20 August, 1780, in *The State Records of North Carolina, Vol. 14*, 568

believed that he was already dead. In fact, with the generous assistance of Lord Rawdon, Porterfield seemed to improve. Although there is no record of his treatment, it is likely that his leg was amputated. That was the common procedure for such a devastating wound as his.

Porterfield was granted his parole by the British days after the battle, but the severity of his injury, and a subsequent illness, kept him in the Camden area for almost five months. Sometime in the winter, however, Porterfield attempted to travel to Charleston, most likely to join his brother, Robert (who was a prisoner in that city). It is unclear how far he got. On the morning of January 10th, 1781, Lieutenant Colonel Charles Porterfield passed away. His brother reported his death to Governor Jefferson.

"I think it my duty to inform Your Excellency, That on the Morning of the 10th [of January] I had the misfortune to loose my Brother (Lieut: Col. Porterfield) on his way from Camden, intending to this place.

I have also to beg leave to mention to Your Excellency, That during my Brother's almost five months extreme illness, The consequence of a wound he received on the 16th of August near Camden, His necessary expenses amounted to a considerable sum; for the purpose of defraying which, he borrowed of Lord Rawden, Thirty Guineas, which I have made myself answerable to his Lordship for, as soon as may be in my power.

My present situation [captive in Charleston] *will point out to your excellency the impossibility of raising such a sum. Therefore, it is that I take the liberty of asking your Excellency's assistance which I flatter myself my Brother's services has merited from the Authority of the State, in whose employ he lost his life."*[21]

What became of Colonel Porterfield is unknown. He lies in an unmarked grave, somewhere in South Carolina -- another forgotten hero of the American Revolution. He was one of the very first Virginians to answer his country's call. He served valiantly at Boston, Quebec, Cooches Bridge, Brandywine, Germantown, Valley Forge, Monmouth, and finally, Camden. Such service and sacrifice clearly validates General Washington's observation, that Charles Porterfield was,

"... universally esteemed by his acquaintances in the Army, as an Officer of very extraordinary Merit."[22]

[21] Robert Porterfield to Governor Jefferson, 1 February, 1781, in *Calendar of Virginia State Papers & Other Manuscripts, Vol. 1*, William P. Palmer, ed., (1875), 479

[22] General Washington to Patrick Henry, 3 October, 1777 in *The Papers of George Washington, Vol. 11*, 375

Bibliography

Adams, John to Elbridge Gerry, 18 June, 1775, *Letters of Delegates to Congress, Vol. 1.* Aug. 1774 – Aug. 1775, (Library of Congress: Online)

Albion Robert and Leonidas Dodson, eds. *Philip Vickers Fithian: Journal, 1775-1776, Written on the Virginia-Pennsylvania Frontier and in the Army Around New York.* Princeton: Princeton University Press, 1934.

Alexander, William. "Letters of William Alexander, Lord Stirling," *Proceedings of the New Jersey Historical Society.* Vol. 60, no. 3 July 1942.

Ballagh, James C. ed., *Letters of Richard Henry Lee, Vol. 1* New York: Macmillan Co., 1911.

Boatner, Mark Mayo, *Encyclopedia of the American Revolution.* New York: D. McKay Co., 1966.

Boyd, Julian P. *The Papers of Thomas Jefferson.* Princeton: Princeton University Press, 1950--

Boyle, Joseph Lee. *Writings from the Valley Forge Encampment of the Continental Army: December 19, 1777 -- June 19, 1778, Vol. 1-2.* Bowie, MD: Heritage Books, 2001.

Buchanan, John. *The Road to Guilford Courthouse: The American Revolution in the Carolina.* John Wiley & Sons, Inc.: NY, 1997.

Campbell, Charles. Ed. "A Sketch of the Military Services Performed by Guilford Dudley, Then of the Town of Halifax, North Carolina, During the Revolutionary War", *Southern Literary Messenger*. Vol. 11, Issues 3-6, 1845. Obtained via the following website: http://battleofcamden.org/dudley.htm

Carrington, Henry B. *Battles of the American Revolution 1775-1781.* New York: A. S. Barnes & Co., 1877.

Cartmell, T. K. *Shenandoah Valley Pioneers and Their Descendants: A History of Frederick County, Virginia,* Winchester, VA, 1909.

Cecere, Michael. *They Behaved Like Soldiers: Captain John Chilton and the Third Virginia Regiment.* Bowie, MD: Heritage Books, 2004.

Chase, Philander D. ed., *The Papers of George Washington: Revolutionary War Series.* Charlottesville: University Press of Virginia, 19

Clark, Stephen. *Following Their Footsteps: A Travel Guide & History of the 1775 Secret Expedition to Capture Quebec.* Clark Books, 2003.

Clark, Walter. ed. "Baron De Kalb, to Major Genl. Gates, 16 July, 1780," *The State Records of North Carolina 1779-1780, Vol. 14.* Winston: M.I. & J.C. Stewart, Printers to the State, 1896.

Commager, Henry Steele and Morris, Richard B., eds. *The Spirit of 'Seventy-Six.* New York: Bobbs-Merrill, 1973.

Cullen, Charles, and Herbert Johnson, eds. *The Papers of John Marshall, Vol. 1.* University of North Carolina Press, 1977.

Dandridge, Danske. "Henry Bedinger to --- Findley", *Historic Shepherdstown.* Charlottesville, VA: Michie Co., 1910.

Dann, John C. *The Revolution Remembered: Eyewitness Accounts of the War Independence.* Chicago: University of Chicago Press, 1980.

Dawson, Henry B. "General Daniel Morgan: An Autobiography" *The Historical Magazine and Notes and Queries Concerning the Antiquities, History and Biography of America.* 2nd Series, Vol. 9. Morrisania, NY, 1871.

Dorman, John. ed. *Virginia Revolutionary Pension Applications, Vols. 1-52*, Washington, D.C.: 1958-95.

Ewald, Johann. *Diary of the American War, A Hessian Journal, Captain Johann Ewald, Field Jaeger Corps.* New Haven and London: Yale University Press, 1979. (Translated and edited by Joseph Tustin)

Fitzpatrick, John C. ed. *The Writings of George Washington from the Original Manuscript Sources, 1745-1799.* (Accessed Online at the Library of Congress under The George Washington Papers)

Fleming, Thomas. *1776: Year of Illusion.* New York: W.W. Norton, 1975.

Flickinger, B. Floyd. "Diary of Lieutenant William Heth while a Prisoner in Quebec, 1776", *Annual Papers of Winchester Virginia Historical Society.* Vol. 1, 1931.

Flickinger, Floyd B. "Captain Morgan and His Riflemen," *Winchester-Frederick County Historical Society Journal.* Vol. 14, 2002.

Force, Peter, ed. *American Archives: 5th Series. 3 vol.* Washington D.C.: U.S. Congress, 1848-1853.

Gates, Horatio. "Horatio Gates, Major General, Commanding Southern Army. Letters and Orders from June 21st to August 31st, 1780", *Magazine of American History.* Vol. 5, No. 4, October, 1880.

Graham, Daniel. *Life of General Daniel Morgan of the Virginia Line of the Army of the United States.* 1856 (Reprint, 1993).

Goodwin, Mary. *Clothing and Accoutrements of the Officers and Soldiers of the Virginia Forces : 1775-1780.* Unpublished, 1962.

Hatch, Robert. *Thrust for Canada: The American Attempt on Quebec in 1775-76.* Boston: Houghton Mifflin, 1979.

Hayes, John. ed., *A Gentleman of Fortune, The Diary of Baylor Hill, First Continental Light Dragoons, 1777-1781, Vol. 2.* Saddlebagg Press, 1995.

Hening, William. *The Statutes at Large being a collection of all the Laws of Virginia from the first session of the Legislature, Vol. 9.* 1821.

Heth, William. "Orderly Book of Major William Heth of the Third (sic) Virginia regiment, May 15 – July 1, 1777", *Virginia Historical Society Collections, New Series, 11* 1892.

Higginbotham, Don. *Daniel Morgan: Revolutionary Rifleman*. Chapel Hill: Univ. of North Carolina Press, 1961.

Jackson, John W. *Valley Forge: Pinnacle of Courage*. Gettysburg, PA: Thomas Publications, 1992.

Johnson, William, "A Narrative of the Campaign of 1781" by Otho Williams in *Sketches of the Life and Correspondence of Nathanael Greene, Vol. 1*. Charleston: A.E. Miller,1822. (Accessed via the Documentary History of the Battle of Camden website at http://battleofcamden.org)

Jordan, John W. ed., "Bethleham During the Revolution, " *Pennsylvania Magazine of History and Biography*. Vol. 12 1888.

Journals of the Continental Congress, 14 June, 1775. Library of Congress Online at www.loc.gov

Kapp, Friedrich. *The Life of Frederick William von Steuben*. NY: Corner house Historical Publications, 1999. (Originally published in 1859)

LaCrosse Jr., Richard. *The Frontier Rifleman*. Union City, TN: Pioneer Press, 1989

Landers, Lieut. Col. H. L. *The Battle of Camden, South Carolina: August 16, 1780*. U.S. Govt. Printing Office: Washington, 1929.

Lee, Charles. *The Lee Papers vol. 1-2*. New York: Collections of the New York Historical Society, 1871.

Lee, Henry. *The Revolutionary War Memoirs of General Henry Lee*. New York: Da Capo Press, 1970, Originally Published in 1812.

Lesser, Charles H. ed., *The Sinews of Independence: Monthly Strength Reports of the Continental Army.* Chicago: University of Chicago Press, 1976.

Marshall, John. *The Life of George Washington, Vol.2.* Fredericksburg, VA: The Citizens' Guild of Washington's Boyhood Home, 1926.

Martin, Joseph Plum. *Private Yankee Doodle.* Edited by George F. Scheer. New York: Little, Brown, 1962.

McGuire, Thomas. *The Surprise of Germantown: October 4th, 1777.* Cliveden of the National Trust for Historic Preservation, 1994.

McIlwaine, H. R. ed. *Journals of the Council of the State of Virginia.* Richmond: Virginia State Library, 1926.

McMichael, James. "The Diary of Lt. James McMichael, of the Pennsylvania Line 1776-1778," *The Pennsylvania Magazine of History and Biography.* Vol. 16, No. 2, 1892.

Montresor, John. "Journal of Captain John Montresor," 3 September, 1777, *The Pennsylvania Magazine of History and Biography.* Vol. 5, Philadelphia: The Historical Society of Pennsylvania, 1881.

Moore, Frank. *Diary of the American Revolution, from Newspapers and Original Documents.* New York: Charles Scribner, 1860. Reprint. New York: New York Times & Arno Press, 1969.

Morrissey, Brendan. *Quebec 1775: The American invasion of Canada.* Osprey, 2003.

Mowday, Bruce E. *September 11, 1777, Washington's Defeat at Brandywine Dooms Philadelphia*. Shippensburg, PA: White Mane Books, 2002.

Palmer, William P. ed. *Calendar of Virginia State Papers & Other Manuscripts, Vol. 1*. 1875.

Pay Roll for Capt. Charles Porterfield's Company of the Eleventh Virginia Regt. Commanded by Col. Daniel Morgan for the Month of May, 1777 in the Manuscript Collection, VA Historical Society, Rec. No.: 132210

Pinckney, Thomas to William Johnson, 27 July, 1822 *Historical Magazine*. Vol 10 No. 8 Aug. 1886. (Accessed via the Documentary History of the Battle of Camden website at http://battleofcamden.org)

Porterfield, Charles. "Diary of Colonel Charles Porterfield," *Magazine of American History* Vol. 21, April 1889.

Posey, John Thornton. General Thomas Posey: *Son of the American Revolution*. East Lansing, MI: Michigan State Univ., 1992.

Powell, Robert. "David Griffith to Major Levin Powell, May 28, 1777" *Biographical Sketch of Col. Levin Powell, 1737 – 1810: Including his Correspondence during the Revolutionary War*. Alexandria. Virginia: G.H. Ramey & Son, 1877.

Reed, John F. *Campaign to Valley Forge: July 1, 1777 – December 19, 1777*. Philadelphia: University of Pennsylvania Press, 1965.

Rees, John. *"What is this you have been about to day?" : The New Jersey Brigade at the Battle of Monmouth.* (Accessed via http://www.revwar75.com in the Complete Works of John U. Rees / New Jersey Brigade)

Roberts, Kenneth. *March to Quebec: Journals of the Members of Arnold's Expedition.* New York: Country Life Press, 1938.

Russell, T. Tripplett and John K. Gott. *Fauquier County in the Revolution.* Westminster, MD : Willow Bend Books, 1988.

Saffell, W.T.R. *Records of the Revolutionary War.* Baltimore: MD, 1894.

Sanchez-Saavedra, E. M. *A Guide to Virginia Military Organizations in the American Revolution : 1774 – 1787.* Richmond : Virginia State Library, 1978.

Scheer, George F., and Hugh F. Rankin. *Rebels & Redcoats: The American Revolution through the Eyes of Those Who Fought and Lived It.* New York: Da Capo Press, 1987.

Scribner, Robert L. and Tarter, Brent (comps). *Revolutionary Virginia: The Road to Independence, volumes 1 thru 7.* Charlottesville: University Press of Virginia, 1978.

Selby, John E. *The Revolution in Virginia : 1775-1783.* New York : Holt Inc., 1996.

Sellers, John R. *The Virginia Continental Line.* Williamsburg: The Virginia Bicentennial Commission, 1978.

Seymour, William. "Journal of the Southern Expedition, 1780-1783", *The Pennsylvania Magazine of History and Biography.* Vol. 7, 1883.

Simcoe, Lt. Col. John. *Simcoe's Military Jouirnal: A History of the Operations of a Partisan Corps Called the Queen's Rangers, Commanded by Lieut. Col. J. G. Simcoe, During the War of Revolution.* New York: New York Times and Arno Press, 1968.

Slaughter, Philip. *A History of St. Mark's Parish : Culpeper County Virginia.* 1877.

Smith, Jean Edward. *John Marshall : Definer of a Nation.* New York : Holt Inc., 1996.

Smith, Samuel. *The Battle of Brandywine.* Monmouth Beach, NJ: Philip Freneau Press, 1976.

Stryker, William. *The Battle of Monmouth.* Princeton: Princeton Univ. Press, 1927.

Sullivan, Thomas. "Before and After the Battle of Brandywine: Extracts from the Journal of Sergeant Thomas Sullivan of H.M. Forty-Ninth Regiment of Foot", 3 September, 1777 *The Pennsylvania Magazine of History and Biography.* Vol. 31, Philadelphia: Historical Society of Pennsylvania, 1907.

Symonds, Craig L. *A Battlefield ATLAS of the American Revolution.* The Nautical & Aviation Publishing Co. of America Inc., 1986.

Tarleton, Banastre, *A History of the Campaigns of 1780 and 1781 in the Southern Provinces of North America.* (reprinted in NY: Arno Press, 1968)

Thacher, James. *A Military Journal during the American Revolutionary War.* Hartford: CT, S. Andrus and Son, 1854. Reprint, New York: Arno Press, 1969.

Townsend, Joseph. "Some Account of the British Army under the Command of General Howe, and of the Battle of Brandywine", *Eyewitness Accounts of the American Revolution.* New York, Arno Press, 1969.

Tyler, Lyon, ed. "The Old Virginia Line in the Middle States During the American Revolution", *Tyler's Quarterly Historical and Genealogical Magazine.* Vol. 12. Richmond, VA: Richmond Press, Inc., Printer, 1931 (Includes: The Diary and Letters of Captain John Chilton)

Uhlendorf, Bernard and Edna Vosper. eds. "Letters of Major Baurmeister During the Philadelphia Campaign," *The Pennsylvania Magazine of History and Biography.* Vol. 59 Philadelphia: Historical Society of Pennsylvania, 1935.

Virginia Gazette. 3 October, 1777, Williamsburg, Printed by Dixon & Hunter.

Virginia Gazette. 19 June, 1779, Williamsburg, Printed by Dixon and Nicholson

Waddell, J. A. "Diary of a Prisoner of War at Quebec, 1776," *Virginia Magazine of History and Biography.* Vol. 9. Richmond, VA: The Virginia Historical Soc., July 1901 no. 1.

Ward, Christopher. *The Delaware Continentals, 1776-1783*. Wilmington, DE: History Society of Delaware, 1941.

Ward, Harry M. *Duty, Honor, or Country : General George Weedon and the American Revolution*. Philadelphia : American Philosophical Society, 1979.

Watts, Garrett. Pension Statement, *Revolutionary Pension Roll, Vol. 14 Sen. Doc. 514, 23rd Cong., 1st ses., 1833-34* (Accessed via the Documentary History of the Battle of Camden website at http://battleofcamden.org)

Weedon, Brigadier General George. Correspondence Account of the Battle of Brandywine, 11 September, 1777. The original manuscript letter is in the collections of the Chicago Historical Society, Transcribed by Bob McDonald, 2001

Willard, Margaret. ed., *Letters on the American Revolution: 1774-1776,* Boston & New York: Houghton Mifflin Co., 1925.

Wright, Robert K. *The Continental Army*. Washington, D.C. Center of Military History: United States Army, 1989.

Index

Brandywine, Battle of 51-79, 152,
Brian, John Oliver, 30
British Grenadiers, 103, 104
British Legion, 114
Brooklyn, 35
Bruin, Peter, 4, 29, 36, 37, 38, 41
Buford, Abraham, 113, 114
Burgoyne, John, 47

C

cadet, 5, 26, 43
Calderwood, James, 38, 41
Cambridge, MA, 8, 13, 14
Camden, SC, 116, 120, 122, 125, 126, 127, 128, 140, 141, 142, 145, 148, 150, 151, 152,
Canada, 10, 11, 12, 36, 47,
Carleton, Governor, 11, 23, 30, 31
Caroline County, 43
Caswell, Gen., 117, 118
Chadd's Ferry, 73
Chadd's Ford, 57, 58, 63, 68, 73, 74, 75
Charleston, SC, 111, 112, 113, 114, 126, 151, 152,
Chesapeake Bay, 47, 48
Chester, NY, 47
Chester, PA, 75
Chew House, 86
Chilton, John, 46, 47, 48,
49, 154, 162
Christianna Creek, 54
Cilley, Joseph, 104
Clevenger, Eden, 38
Clinton, George, 96
Clinton, Henry, 99, 101, 111
Colburn, Reuben, 13, 14
Combs Hill, 103
Concord, MA, 1
Congress, 1, 2, 3, 9, 35, 36, 44, 55, 66, 77, 81, 85, 88, 91, 92, 99,
Cooches Bridge, 52, 53, 54, 55, 152
Cornwallis, Lord, 122, 127, 142, 146, 149

D

De Kalb, Baron, 114, 115, 116, 148, 149,
Dead River, 16, 17
Dearborn, Henry, 29
Deep River, 115
Delaware Continentals, 144, 144
Delaware River, 47, 88
Dillworth, PA, 75, 76
Drew, Captain, 127, 131, 132, 143
Dudley, Guilford, 5, 126, 127, 129, 136, 144,
Dunore, Lord, 1,

J

Jefferson, Thomas, 109, 110, 111, 114, 115, 146
Johnson, William, 37, 41

K

Kennebeck River, 11, 13, 14, 15, 16
Kennett Meetinghouse, 60
Kennett Square, 58, 59
King William Co., 110
Knyphausen, Gen., 59, 60, 62, 63, 65, 66, 72, 73, 74, 75

L

Laurens, Henry, 92, 93, 103
Lee, Charles, 100, 101, 102
Lee, Richard Henry, 6,
Lincoln, Benjamin, 113
Little Lynches Creek, 120, 121
Lockhart, Capt., 130
Long, Gabriel, 38, 41, 59, 76, 77
Loudoun County, 37, 38, 41

M

Maleen, Doctor, 31
Manhattan, 35
Marshall, John, 37, 51, 66, 76, 79, 80, 88, 95, 98,

Marshall, Thomas, 68, 72, 83, 112
Martin, Joseph Plum, 91, 92,
Maryland Continentals, 114
Maxwell's Light Corps, 51, 52, 54, 56, 58, 59, 65, 66, 67, 68, 74, 79, 80, 81, 82, 83
Maxwell, William, 51, 52, 53, 54, 55, 56, 58, 59, 63, 64, 65, 66, 67, 72, 74, 75, 79, 80, 81, 82, 83, 100
McClanachan, Alexander, 83
McMichael, James, 76
Moncton, Henry, 103
Monmouth, Battle of, 98, 99, 101, 102, 105, 106, 107, 152,
Montgomery, Richard, 12, 22, 23, 24, 27, 29, 30, 36
Montressor, John, 52, 53, 55, 56
Morgan, Daniel, 3, 4, 5, 7, 8, 14, 15, 19, 21, 22, 25, 26, 27, 28, 29, 30, 35, 36, 37, 38, 40, 41, 43, 44, 45, 46, 60, 64, 82, 93, 94, 95, 100, 101, 107, 108,
Morgan's Musket Regt., 38
Morgan's Rifle Corps, 45, 46, 95, 101, 107

Rutledge, John, 114

S

Saratoga, Battle of, 46, 93
Saunders Creek, 144
Scammell, Alexander, 96
Schuyler, Philip, 11, 12
Schuylkill River, 82, 91
Scott, Charles, 91, 100, 101
Senf, Lt. Col., 125
Senter, Isaac, 18, 19, 20, 21
Seymour, William, 148
Sheperdstown, MD, 4, 7,
Shippen, William, 39
Simms, Lt. Col., 58, 62
Skowhegan, ME, 16
Slaughter, Philip, 95, 161
Smith, William, 37, 41,
South Carolina, 47, 110, 111, 112, 113, 114, 116, 120, 139, 149, 152
St. Lawrence River, 21, 22, 23, 27
Stephen, Adam, 44, 68, 85, 86, 130,
Stephenson, Hugh, 3, 35
Steuben, Baron von, 97-98
Stevens, Edward, 122, 123, 144, 146, 147
Stewart, Walter, 102
Stirling, William, 68, 94, 95, 104, 108,
Stocking, Abner, 14, 16

Stothard, Thomas, 38
Sullivan, John, 68, 69, 84, 85, 86
Sullivan, Thomas, 53, 56, 62, 64, 67, 73, 74
Sussex Court House, NJ, 7
Sutfin House, 104
Sutton's Plantation, 128

T

Tarleton, Banastre, 114, 122, 128, 129, 130,
Thacher, James, 8
Thayer, Simon, 16
Thompson, Col., 13
Tracy, Nathaniel, 12, 13
Trenton, NJ, 43, 84

V

Valley Forge, 81, 89, 91, 93, 96, 99, 152,
Varnum, James, 92
Virginia Board of War, 111
Virginia State Council, 37, 40
Virginia State Garrison Regiment, 106, 109, 110, 112
Volunteers of Ireland, 120

W

Waggoner, Peter, 60, 66
Warwick, PA, 81

ABOUT THE AUTHOR

MICHAEL CECERE SR. is the proud father of two incredible children, Jenny and Michael Jr., and a grateful husband to Susan Cecere. He teaches American History at Robert E. Lee High School in Fairfax County, Virginia and is entering his 13th year as a public school teacher. He also teaches American History and American Government (part time) at Northern Virginia Community College. He holds a Master of Arts degree in History and another in Political Science. An avid Revolutionary and Civil War re-enactor, he participates in numerous living history events and demonstrations throughout the year. He contributes articles to the Brigade of the American Revolution, as well as to the newsletters of his re-enacting units, the 3rd and 7th Virginia Regiments. He is also the editor of the 7th Virginia's newsletter. Currently he is conducting research on another forgotten patriot, Lt. Col. Charles Porterfield of Frederick County, Virginia.